BEYOND THE BADGE

CRIME, JUSTICE, AND
THE FBI IN THAILAND

BEYOND THE BADGE

JOHN SCHACHNOVSKY

COPYRIGHT © 2025 JOHN SCHACHNOVSKY
All rights reserved.

BEYOND THE BADGE
Crime, Justice, and the FBI in Thailand

FIRST EDITION

ISBN 978-1-5445-4848-7   *Hardcover*
      978-1-5445-4847-0   *Paperback*
      978-1-5445-4846-3   *Ebook*
      978-1-5445-5019-0   *Audiobook*

For my late father, who dedicated his life to security and intelligence and always encouraged me to pursue my best.

Thanks to him, I found my way to the FBI, and it's truly the greatest job in the world.

I hope I made him proud.

CONTENTS

FOREWORD 9
PROLOGUE 13

1. WHAT IS AN FBI LEGAT? 17
2. HOW DID I GET HERE? 31
3. WHERE AM I? 53
4. THE DEATH OF DAVID CARRADINE 71
5. TICK TICK BOOM 83
6. THE MARINE 99
7. NOWHERE TO RUN 115
8. WHITE-COLLAR CRIME 133
9. LAOS AND MYANMAR 147
10. BODY PARTS 167

BUCKSHOT 187
ACKNOWLEDGMENTS 203
ABOUT THE AUTHOR 205

FOREWORD

— JIRABHOP BHURIDEJ,
POLICE LIEUTENANT GENERAL,
CENTRAL INVESTIGATION
BUREAU, ROYAL THAI POLICE

I AM VERY PLEASED AND HONORED TO INTRODUCE THIS exciting book authored by my friend and colleague John Schachnovsky, a retired FBI agent who dedicated a large part of his career to service in Thailand. As one of the leaders in the Royal Thai Police, I have the privilege of recognizing John and the invaluable contributions and expertise he shared with the Thai law enforcement community.

After reading about John's time in Thailand, readers will gain a unique perspective on law enforcement in the country, as seen through the eyes of a veteran FBI agent. The experiences not only reveal the complexities of policing in our nation but also serve as a testament to the power of collaboration and partnership between law enforcement agencies across borders.

The collaboration John and I shared on multiple occasions is a testament to the importance of exchanging expertise and learning from one another in our shared mission to uphold justice and maintain peace.

The bond between the FBI and the Royal Thai Police highlights the camaraderie and respect that unite law enforcement professionals worldwide. It is through such collaborations that we expand our horizons and enhance our ability to combat crime and protect our communities effectively.

To John, who dedicated his career to serving in Thailand, I extend my deepest gratitude for your unwavering commitment to excellence and your tireless efforts in upholding the principles of justice and integrity. Your experiences and insights shared in this book will undoubtedly inspire and educate people in Thailand, the United States, and beyond.

I am confident that this book will serve as a source of inspiration and learning for all those who have chosen the path of law enforcement. May it remind us of the importance of cooperation, understanding, and continuous learning as we strive to make our communities safer and more secure.

With the utmost respect and admiration.

PROLOGUE

THE SONY CORPORATION HACK

DO YOU REMEMBER THE MOVIE *THE INTERVIEW*, STARring Seth Rogen and James Franco? It was a dark comedy that took aim at North Korea, with a fictional plot to assassinate Kim Jong-Un.

And it was responsible for one of the biggest cyberattacks of the decade.

In November of 2014, Sony Pictures got hit by a group calling themselves the "Guardians of Peace." They went all in: they hacked Sony's network and leaked everything from employee details and unreleased movies to the private emails of top execs. It was massive and not the kind of thing that could be swept under the rug. The implications were financial and personal—and humiliating for the company.

Sony was getting hit from all angles. The hackers also threatened to commit acts of violence at theaters planning to show the film, leading Sony to scrap its release entirely. The whole thing turned into a national security issue. At this point, the FBI got involved and linked the hack to North Korea, though the North Korean government completely denied involvement.

As it turned out, some of the leaks were traced back to the St. Regis Hotel in Bangkok. Random, but that's where I came in.

Drawn to the FBI and Thailand

Before I get into any more details, I'm going to tell you a little more about me.

I am a former FBI Special Agent who was assigned to work in Bangkok, Thailand. My official title was FBI Legal Attache, legat for short (I'll tell you more about that role in Chapter 1). Law enforcement is in my blood. Growing up, my father worked as a US Marshal and later had a long career with the National Security Agency (NSA).

I didn't originally plan to follow in his footsteps; I was focused on sports and even thought about pursuing a master's degree in that field. But after some not-so-subtle nudges from him and an unforgettable chat with a cop at a college party, I found myself drawn to the work.

I can remember multiple conversations with my dad where he painted the world of government work as stable and rewarding, one defined by pride in the job, genuine satisfaction, solid compensation, and long-term security. Every time the economy took a nosedive, he reminded me that government salaries were mostly safe from market crashes. And during our nightly national-news-watching ritual, he'd always point out how his work was somehow connected to what was happening in the world.

But the biggest thing? Dad genuinely loved his job. He was always happy to go to work; he never, ever complained. That was something you didn't see often back then, and you still don't today.

Eventually, I joined the FBI, and after a few years stateside, I found myself pulled to Thailand. I'd fallen for the country and its culture during a short-term work assignment, and I knew right away that I wanted to come back. The moment I set foot in Thailand on my first visit, I felt like it was home.

I served with the FBI in Thailand for 10 years, from 2008 to 2019, navigating a new language, bridging cultural divides, and building partnerships with Thai police and agencies from around the world.

Cracking one of the most infamous hacks of the decade

I was about six years into my role as Legat Bangkok when I was asked to help with the Sony Corporation hack. My job? To find the computer used in the hacking operation, grab it, and ship it to the FBI cybersecurity team in LA. I walked into the hotel and explained what I needed, and to my surprise, without even a hard sell, they were immediately cooperative. Turned out they already knew about the hack.

The hotel staff handed over the computer (it was a desktop), wrapped in a plastic bag, right there in the lobby. We kept it casual, no suits or badges, nothing to draw attention. Just me, my Thai police colleague, and the hotel's tech equipment walking out the front door.

I brought the computer back to my office in the US Embassy, got it securely packaged up, and shipped it off to the case agents in LA. That computer became a solid piece of evidence in cracking one of the FBI's most infamous hacking cases.

My work on this case in particular is only the tip of the iceberg. I was involved in the David Carradine case (the famous *Kill Bill* actor who was found dead in a Bangkok hotel) and coordinated details between police agencies during the Erawan Shrine bombing investigation. I've helped extradite murderers and escort fugitives across international borders. I've worked cases in the highly secretive and difficult-to-navigate countries of Laos and Myanmar too.

And I've helped identify murder victims.

I have had an incredible career with the FBI in Thailand. This book is my way of sharing some of the stories of the cases I worked on, my deep respect for the Kingdom of Thailand, and the power of international cooperation.

CHAPTER 1

WHAT IS AN FBI LEGAT?

MY JOURNEY INTO THE WORLD OF INTERNATIONAL LAW enforcement as Legat Bangkok began in December of 2008. Little did I know it would lead to some of the most intense cases of my entire career.

One of them was the extradition of a Mozambique fugitive in 2018.

I remember the moment vividly. I was already deeply entrenched in my role as Legat Bangkok. My job often crossed borders, but nothing quite prepared me for the call that came from Legat Pretoria, South Africa, who covered multiple countries, including Mozambique. The Mozambique Attorney General's Office had reached out, seeking FBI assistance in apprehending a notorious fugitive, Momade Assif Abdul Satar.

Satar had a reputation that extended beyond borders. He was wanted for more than 50 kidnapping-for-ransom cases and murder.

The twist? Satar wasn't hiding in Mozambique. He was believed to be in Thailand. It is important to explain that while many countries have embassies in Thailand, not all have a law enforcement presence, and some don't even have formal treaties in place related to police cooperation. Mozambique fit the latter description, so the Mozambique authorities enlisted the FBI to assist with the Satar case.

When the legat in Pretoria contacted me, she asked for my help. Tracking down Satar was priority number one for the Attorney General's Office in Mozambique.

Satar had been living a life of deception in Thailand, having entered the country with a fake passport under the alias Sahime Mohammad Aslam three years prior to his eventual capture. Before his time in Thailand, Satar was freed on parole from a Mozambique prison, where he was convicted of the gangland-style murder of an investigative journalist in Maputo in 2000.

Interpol had issued a Red Notice (a request to law enforcement worldwide to locate and provisionally arrest a person pending extradition, or in the case of Satar, potential deportation), alleging that Satar masterminded a string of kidnappings not only in Mozambique but also across several other African countries, all from the safety of his hideout in Thailand. His gang was responsible for kidnapping over 50 wealthy businessmen, demanding ransoms as high as $3M for their release. Tragically, two of his victims were murdered during this reign of terror.

The Mozambique officials were nervous and desperate, knowing that Satar's powerful connections could thwart any overt attempts to capture him. Issuing a Red Notice was the first and most important step to begin to secure Thailand's assistance.

According to the officials I met with, Satar had deep connections at the highest levels of the Mozambique government. They were certain his powerful allies would quickly learn that his presence in Thailand had been discovered. The officials expressed their concern that Satar would be tipped off, giving him the opportunity to evade capture once again, as he had done in the past. This added an extra layer of urgency to the operation; any misstep could result in him slipping through our fingers before we even had the chance to close in.

And so began a high-stakes, discreet operation. I carefully coordinated with my counterparts in Thailand, leveraging every bit of trust and goodwill I had built over the years (this was a critical part of the job as a legat, something I learned early on). Calling in favors wasn't a decision to be taken lightly, but Satar was a dangerous man, and lives were on the line.

With the information about Satar utilizing a fake passport, the Thai police were able to identify an address where Satar was supposedly hiding. Unfortunately, this turned out to be a dead end.

The Thai police continued to review all the information they had, but still there was no trace of Satar and no guarantee he would be found.

But, as I have witnessed time and time again, the Royal Thai Police (RTP) are highly skilled, and in this case, their reputation for thoroughness proved true once again. Despite the initial dead ends, the RTP diligently tracked down Satar and verified his location.

A breakthrough in the case

The Mozambique officials traveled to Thailand to apprehend Satar and bring him back home, but it wasn't that easy. Communication between the two countries was critical for this to work, and the language barrier became a serious challenge.

The focus of the investigation had shifted. It wasn't about finding Satar anymore; the Thais already knew his whereabouts. The concern now was about communicating the vital details Mozambique officials had gathered about Satar and why he was wanted and outlining a plan to bring him to justice.

I leveraged my strong working relationship with the RTP to help them understand that Satar was a dangerous individual who needed to be brought to justice and that I needed their help verifying whether he was living in Thailand. I did this without sharing too many specifics of the case. They trusted me, and they trusted that the FBI agent in Pretoria wouldn't make the request unless it truly mattered.

But that was as far as we could go. Once we confirmed that Satar was in Thailand, it was up to the Mozambique officials to present their case in full detail and convince the Thai authorities to actually take him into custody and begin the complex process of removal, especially difficult without an extradition treaty in place.

At the same time, the Thai officials needed to explain their protocols, what the arrest operation would entail, and what specific paperwork or requirements they needed from Mozambique to move forward.

The next step was to get everyone in the same room and iron out all the details. The setting for the meeting was far from glamorous. We sat in high wooden chairs, the room devoid of any amenities or air conditioning, with only low-level staff bringing in the occasional tea or coffee. Despite the stark environment, trust was the currency in that room. I had built strong relationships with my counterparts over the years, and the RTP trusted me to represent their interests with officials from a government they had never worked with. At the same time, my RTP colleagues also put faith in me that I would be straight with them when I explained Mozambique's interests. Finally, the Mozambique officials were in a strange land, and they trusted that I would be able to help them get what they wanted. It was one of the many "how did I get myself in this situation?" types of moments.

When we first sat down, RTP needed to know exactly what the Mozambique officials wanted. They had located

Satar, the first step in making sure the Mozambique officials weren't wasting their time by flying to Thailand. But the actual arrest, taking a man into custody with the intent of sending him back to face justice, required hard evidence. When the Thai police investigator began to ask the Mozambique officials to lay out the facts, I immediately knew we had a problem. The Mozambique officials, with their thick accents, were difficult to understand, and as soon as the Mozambique official started to explain the situation, the Thai police all looked at me.

I was perplexed at what they wanted from me. I was already thinking about how long I needed to stay in the meeting. At that point, I had done my job.

The Thais had found Satar.

The Mozambique officials had arrived.

I had set up the meeting.

All things considered, they really shouldn't *need me anymore.*

But when my Thai police colleague gave me a quizzical look, I realized he couldn't understand what the Mozambique official was saying. I repeated, word for word, what the Mozambique official said, and the Thai police all nodded their heads. They took a minute or so to talk among themselves, in Thai, formulating a response. They responded, in English, and explained some of the steps they would take to help the Mozambique officials get the result they wanted.

Immediately after the Thai official finished, the Mozambique officials looked at me with the exact same puzzled look the Thais had given me a few minutes earlier. I looked at the Mozambique officials, then turned to the Thai officials.

I paused for a moment and then said, "Just so we are all

clear on this, all of you are speaking English. I am doing an English-to-English translation at the moment."

I expected a response that would allow me to excuse myself. "Thank you for clarifying things, John. You're free to go." However, what I received was a look, from all parties, that told me they knew exactly what was happening and they fully expected me to continue in the new role as their translator for as long as I was needed

We all shared a laugh at the irony of the situation, and to this day, I am pretty sure the laugh was at my expense.

I was confident the RTP could arrest Satar and send him back to Mozambique, but Mozambique had to explain the reasoning behind the manhunt and why it was crucial to bring him there. It was important to make the Thai authorities see this as more than just another arrest. This was about removing a dangerous criminal from Thailand.

It also had to be ensured that the Thai officials were clear on everything they needed from Mozambique: paperwork, procedures, and the like. Without an extradition treaty in place, this operation would be treated as a deportation. Fortunately, Satar's Interpol Red Notice made the process more straightforward, since he was an internationally wanted man. That Red Notice was our ace in the hole, allowing the operation to proceed with minimal obstacles.

The meeting, while not the smoothest of diplomatic endeavors (turns out even English-to-English translation has some serious nuance), was a success, and the Thai police arrested Satar without incident soon after they were satisfied with the information provided.

But our job wasn't done yet. The Mozambique officials needed to be in control of what happened next: they wanted to bring Satar to justice on their own soil. He needed to be deported. So we navigated bureaucratic hurdles and secured the necessary approvals. As we waited for the final clearance, I could tell everyone was worried. We were so close, but approval wasn't a foregone conclusion.

Deputy Prime Minister Prawit Wongsuwan gave the green light for Pol Maj Gen Surachate Hakpan, the Commander of the Thai Tourist Police, to take charge of the case. "Big Joke," as he is affectionately known, was an invaluable friend and contact for the FBI in Thailand. His connection with the FBI runs deep, as he graduated from the prestigious FBI National Academy (FBINA), a professional training course for US and international law enforcement managers nominated by their agency heads due to demonstrated leadership qualities. The program is extremely selective, and the RTP officers chosen for the FBINA are honored to go and become lifelong members of the FBI family. Many senior RTP officers, including multiple Chiefs of Police, have been FBINA graduates. Big Joke's understanding of international law enforcement collaboration made him the perfect partner for handling this complex case. While Big Joke ran into some unfortunate legal issues in the latter stages of his career, ending his tenure with the Royal Thai Police earlier then he would have hoped, I will always have fond memories of working with him and our mutual respect among trusted colleagues.

Finally, the call came: the green light to proceed. Shortly afterward, I escorted the Mozambique officials to the detention center where Satar awaited deportation.

Satar was deported on July 30, 2018, marking the culmination of weeks of intense effort and collaboration. Throughout the case, I couldn't help but marvel at the teamwork between nations. Here we were, Mozambique,

Thailand, and the US, working together to tackle a problem, the capture and extradition of a dangerous criminal, that transcended borders. It was a reminder of the importance of international cooperation in the fight against crime.

Why legats matter

The FBI was founded in 1908. On July 26, 1908, Attorney General Charles J. Bonaparte took a pivotal step by appointing an unnamed force of special agents to serve as the investigative arm of the Department of Justice. This small group would eventually evolve into what we know today as the FBI.

At the time, the DOJ had no investigative force of its own and had been relying on agents borrowed from the US Secret Service. They needed an independent investigative unit to handle the increasing complexity of federal cases. This need became the driving force behind the creation of the FBI.

Then, during World War II, President Roosevelt recognized the need for international intelligence operations. South and Central America were becoming hotbeds for Nazi espionage, with spies using these regions as staging grounds to infiltrate the US and relay intelligence back to Germany. President Roosevelt turned to the FBI to address this growing threat.

In response, the FBI established a Special Intelligence Service in June of 1940, sending agents undercover to disrupt the Nazi spy network. Around this same time, the FBI began officially stationing agents as diplomatic liaisons in US embassies.

By the end of 1942, special agents had also been assigned to US embassies in cities like Bogotá and London. These agents held the title of Legal Attachés, commonly referred to as "legats."[1]

A legat is a critical figure in the FBI. We are tasked with representing the agency in foreign countries. We are essential for coordinating international investigations, many of which stem from the Bureau's overseas intelligence work.

The introduction of the legat marked the beginning of the FBI's global reach.

Over the years, the legat program expanded, evolving into a network of offices and suboffices, currently numbering around 90 worldwide.

How does one become a legat?

Becoming a legat is voluntary, meaning agents are not automatically assigned but must apply and compete for the position. A legat is a very special assignment, with every overseas vacancy receiving a large number of applicants for very few positions. Out of approximately 14,000 agents in the FBI, only a few hundred are stationed overseas at any given time.

The process starts after agents graduate from the FBI Academy and are assigned to one of 55 field offices. If they're interested in opportunities abroad, they can apply for openings in the legat or ALAT (Assistant Legal Attache) positions. These roles typically open up about 18 months in advance, allowing time for the application and training process. Once assigned, agents undergo specific training and prepare to relocate, often moving their families to their new posts. In

---

[1] "History of Legal Attachés," Federal Bureau of Investigation, accessed June 26, 2025, https://www.fbi.gov/history/history-of-legal-attaches.

some cases, emergencies may expedite the process, but usually, it's a well-planned and structured transition.

What do legats do?

So what exactly do legats do overseas? We serve as the FBI's representatives in the countries where we are stationed, and in some cases, we are also responsible for other surrounding countries where there is no FBI representation. We act as liaisons between the FBI and local law enforcement agencies, sharing intelligence, coordinating investigations, and facilitating cooperation on cases that cross international borders.

Our responsibilities are multifaceted. The FBI investigates over 300 different types of violations, and the nature of the work varies depending on the country where the legat is stationed. In some places, the focus might be more on counterterrorism, while in others, cybercrime takes center stage. In Bangkok, we dealt with a bit of everything: white-collar crime, cybercrime, counterterrorism, and, most importantly, coverage of investigative leads for domestic agents back in the US. We handled a wide range of cases, assisting FBI offices at home with international aspects of their investigations, no matter the type of crime.

From tracking down fugitives like Satar, who fled Mozambique, to investigating cybercrimes with international connections, legats are at the forefront of combating transnational crime.

One important difference between working domestically and working internationally is the specific law enforcement powers officers and agents possess. Foreign police officers retain very few of the powers they have domestically when they work in overseas assignments. Specifically, the power to arrest an individual, even one of your same nationality, is not authorized. For all arrests, search warrants, and other court-ordered law enforcement actions, legats are required to utilize the assistance of the local police to carry out their duties. This is the same for all police agencies all over the world. There are some exceptions, including countries officially deputizing foreign police to allow for the physical arrest made by non-citizen police officers, but these exceptions are rare.

Capacity building is a significant aspect of a legat's work too: legats work closely with foreign law enforcement agencies and provide training and assistance to help build their ability to handle complex cases. In countries where resources are limited, legats help train local police forces and enhance their investigative capabilities.

In other countries, capacity building isn't as prevalent because the relationship is more of an equal partnership. However, the FBI is widely regarded as being at the forefront of law enforcement globally. Even in countries where resources aren't limited, our agents still provide training on new investigative techniques and emerging trends. This ensures that even the most well-equipped agencies stay updated with the latest developments in crime-fighting strategies, strengthening our partnerships and enhancing cooperation worldwide.

Legats also play a crucial role in diplomatic relations. We serve as key members of the US Embassy community, briefing ambassadors and other government officials on FBI matters. We collaborate with various government agencies on issues ranging from political instability to humanitarian efforts.

Why are legats important?

The spread of the internet and global banking has made money laundering easier and more widespread. With the rise of cryptocurrency, tracking illicit funds has become even more challenging for law enforcement. Terrorist groups can now recruit and gain members globally with relative ease. The interconnected world we live in today has made everyday life more convenient, but that convenience extends to criminals as well. This is where legats play a critical role. They are already stationed around the world, and their presence is essential in addressing this new front line of criminal activity, which directly impacts the United States. Legats are on the ground, working to counter these evolving threats in real time.

By empowering these international agencies to tackle crime effectively, the FBI strengthens its global network of allies in the fight against terrorism, organized crime, and other threats.

The importance of having legats stationed in foreign countries cannot be overstated. We provide invaluable insights and connections that are vital for responding swiftly to international crises, such as terrorist attacks or natural disasters, that involve American citizens abroad. Our presence ensures that the FBI maintains a proactive approach to combating threats on a global scale, safeguarding national security interests wherever they may arise.

A global network of law enforcement

The case of Momade Assif Abdul Satar serves as a vivid example of the power and necessity of international cooperation in law enforcement. It was not just about one man's capture; it was a demonstration of how the FBI, working in partnership with law enforcement agencies across the globe, can dismantle networks of crime that transcend borders. The successful extradition of Satar highlights the critical role that legats play in connecting countries, navigating complex legal systems, and ensuring that justice is served no matter where the criminals are hiding.

As Legat Bangkok, my job required a blend of diplomacy, cultural awareness, and investigative expertise. I wasn't just tracking down fugitives; I was building bridges between nations, fostering trust, and facilitating the kind of collaboration that makes cases like Satar's possible. The work is challenging, often unpredictable, and always high stakes. But when you see someone like Satar brought to justice, it becomes clear why legats are essential to the FBI's mission of protecting the United States, and the world, from those who seek to do harm.

Ultimately, the role of a legat is about more than just solving individual cases. It's about strengthening a global network of law enforcement, making sure that no matter how international crime evolves, the FBI will be ready to respond swiftly and effectively. The capture of Satar was just one victory in a much larger battle, but it underscores the profound impact that legats can have on keeping our world safer.

Now that you know what an FBI legat is and does, let's talk about how I made it to Thailand.

CHAPTER 2

HOW DID I GET HERE?

GROWING UP, MY DAD WAS DEEPLY ROOTED IN LAW enforcement. He worked as a local sheriff and police officer near his hometown in upstate New York, then as a Deputy US Marshal. After that, he worked with the New York State Liquor Authority for the State of New York and was then recruited by NSA. Naturally, I was surrounded by stories of his career, but I had my sights set on something different. I wanted to pursue sports, and seriously considered getting my master's degree in the field.

My dad, however, had a different suggestion: why not try law enforcement?

For most of my early life, I was determined not to follow in his footsteps. I wanted to carve my own path, and law enforcement didn't seem like it was for me. But there was always this thought in the back of my mind: if all else fails, I could always do what Dad did.

I grew up in Columbia, Maryland, right between Baltimore and Washington, not too far from NSA headquarters. It was a great spot, with easy access to both cities.

My sister went to Union College, a small liberal arts college in upstate New York. I wasn't really sure where I wanted to attend college, but I had played ice hockey almost my entire childhood, and with Union having a good hockey program, I ended up attending Union as well. Getting there was a bit of a trek from Columbia, about an eight-hour drive or a two-hour flight, but it was worth it for the experiences I had there. I played on the JV hockey team, hoping to eventually make it to varsity. (I never did. I shattered my kneecap at the end of my sophomore year, which ended my college hockey career.)

One night during college, at a party hosted by my fraternity, we hired a cop for security to watch the door. While my friends were partying inside, I spent the whole night hanging out with the cop, just BSing and talking shop. I remember standing outside the fraternity house, listening to the officer talk about crime in the local area, his daily routine, the satisfaction he got from the job, and the excitement he felt going to work every day. And I recall getting more and more intrigued by the work of the police as the discussion continued for hours. It hit me then, and I embraced the idea of exploring a career in law enforcement. Union was a liberal arts school where most students went on to become doctors or lawyers, but here I was, realizing that maybe law enforcement was where I was meant to be all along. That was when I knew: I wanted to be a cop.

Stepping into law enforcement

As I continued at Union, working in law enforcement went from an idea to something I began to actively pursue. As friends discussed plans to work in business or law, I knew I couldn't sit behind a desk all day. When I talked to my dad about my newfound appreciation for the profession, he reiterated his reasoning for law enforcement as a career choice. He always loved his work, and seeing that passion made me want what he had: a career that felt meaningful and fulfilling. Also, growing up in the DC area, you're constantly surrounded by people in service, whether it's law enforcement, intelligence, or government work. It becomes a part of the environment, almost like second nature, and you start to understand the importance of these roles.

That sense of duty and service was always around me, even if I didn't recognize it at first.

My law enforcement career started when I joined the

ranks of the Border Patrol in 1994, I embraced the rigor of a militaristic academy. The Border Patrol Academy was at the Federal Law Enforcement Training Center, or FLETC for short, in Glynco, Georgia.

Every day in uniform came with its own set of challenges. We had to make sure the brass on our uniforms was polished and our boots were spotless. Each morning began with a lineup, where we stood at "parade rest" to listen to announcements. We weren't allowed to move, no matter what.

Being in southern Georgia brought with it some things that I will never forget. For example, I remember the sand fleas were the worst: biting our faces while we stood at attention, knowing that swatting them away would earn us a round of pushups. To avoid that, many of us slathered our faces in Skin So Soft to keep the bugs at bay. Physical training was intense, with regular runs in formation. It was tough, but it taught us discipline and built a strong sense of camaraderie.

Those years instilled in me invaluable lessons in diligence and dedication; they shaped my character for the better. I then worked as a Border Patrol Agent and lived in Sierra Vista, Arizona, until 1997, when I relocated to Chicago.

After a couple of years in the Border Patrol, I realized that while the job was exciting and meaningful, I wanted to move to a job that was more investigative.

I was working on the Border Patrol's Mountain Bike Patrol Unit when the US Attorney General (AG) visited our patrol station. The AG at the time was Janet Reno, and one of the events on her schedule was to meet my bike patrol team, as we were a newer unit in the station. That meeting gave me an opportunity to meet one of the FBI agents on her protective detail, and it was that encounter that changed the trajectory of my law enforcement career. He asked me if I was planning on being in the Border Patrol my entire career or if I would consider applying to the FBI. Before this conversation, the FBI was for me what I assumed it was for most everyone: a cool job I only saw in the movies.

After I met with the agent, I went back to my apartment and called my dad.

"Dad, do you think I have a chance of making it into the FBI?"

"I really haven't thought much about it, John, because I've been focused on your success with the Border Patrol. But I support the decision. I think it's a great idea!"

I needed to have three years of work experience before I was eligible to apply to the FBI. The day I finished my third year, I did just that.

In the meantime, as there were no guarantees that the FBI would hire me, I also applied for other criminal investigator jobs. I had decided to take the first investigator job offered to me because I wanted to learn the job of an investigator sooner rather than later. I was hired to be a Special Agent for the US Department of Commerce, so I moved to Chicago. This is a smaller agency that is primarily tasked with combating illegal exports.

After arriving in Chicago, I was sent back to FLETC for an eight-week criminal investigator academy to prepare for the Commerce position. Then I returned to Chicago to begin work as an agent. The job involved monitoring illegal dual-use exports, goods that could have both civilian and military applications, to countries like Iran, Iraq, Syria, Cuba, and North Korea.

At FLETC, I met my wife, who was pursuing her passion for forensic science. She was doing an internship there while working towards her master's degree in forensic science at George Washington University. Two years later, we were married.

Chicago was home for only a couple of years. All the while, I was going through the FBI's very long hiring process. It took months to hear back after the initial written test. I had the same experience after I interviewed.

Then, in July of 1999, a few weeks after our wedding, I was accepted into the FBI and moved to Quantico, Virginia.

The FBI Academy

In the scorching summer of 1999, Quantico became my temporary home. At the time, to qualify as an FBI agent, candidates needed a college degree and to meet one of several criteria: fluency in a second language, a law degree, an accounting degree, or a diversified background, which meant three years of experience in law enforcement, the military, or other critical fields. The FBI was always looking for the best and brightest, so a diverse background was key to building a strong FBI workforce. This push for diversity was evident when looking at some of the Agents I met over the years. For example, one of my colleagues in the San Francisco Field Office had been a sushi chef prior to joining the FBI.

The skills they're looking for change all the time. My time with the Border Patrol and US Department of Commerce satisfied the service requirement.

Becoming an FBI Special Agent is one of the most grueling application processes there is, not just in law enforcement or the US government, but in all fields worldwide. Qualifying to apply is only the first step.

After you are told your basic qualifications are "good enough" to apply, a written test is the next step. If successful, you go through an interview with three current Special Agents. Each of these testing phases weeds out tens of thousands of applicants. If you pass the interview, you are given a "conditional appointment" as a Special Agent.

The conditions? Passing a physical fitness test, a medical evaluation, a polygraph exam, and a background investigation for any questionable activity from the time you turned 18 years old until the present day.

After all of that, you need to make it through the FBI Academy. Then, and only then, can you be called an FBI Special Agent.

When I arrived in Quantico, I have to admit I was a little intimidated. Like everyone else, I only knew the FBI from pop culture. While many of us may have come across FBI Agents in our previous jobs, the academy felt like hallowed ground, and I knew graduating was going to be one of the biggest challenges of my life.

I was assigned a dorm room and roommate who was in my class. We got along very well and often stayed up late studying together. We did lots of typical random roommate types of things. While he didn't become my closest friend at the academy, I can say he was a great roommate and helped me make it through the academy with our daily conversations about classes and work-life balance and the constant motivation we gave each other. Everyone in my class lived on the same two floors of the dorm, which fostered a deep sense of unity as we navigated the challenges of training.

The FBI Academy was a completely different experience compared to the Border Patrol and Commerce academies. The Border Patrol academy was highly militaristic: former

Marines even said it reminded them of the Marine Corps. Every day, aside from the meticulous inspection of your uniform, we had a strict routine that included running with our class flag. It was a real wake-up call for a fraternity hockey player like me, but it was where I truly grew up and became the man I am today, with values of honor, respect, and discipline deeply instilled.

The Commerce academy was much more low-key. The criminal investigator class was only eight weeks long. It covered the basics with a bit of firearms training, but nothing too intense. After my Border Patrol experience, I aced it all without much difficulty.

The FBI Academy, though, is on a whole different level. It's like the Harvard of law enforcement training. The FBI is considered the premier law enforcement agency in the world, and the academy reflects that. Just like Harvard Law's portrayal in the bestselling book *One L*, they push you hard, but there's a sense of prestige because you've been selected from thousands of applicants. Even internationally, agencies like the Thai police view the FBI as the gold standard in law enforcement, and the academy experience reinforces that reputation.

Also, unlike the Border Patrol dormitories, the academy offered comfort amid a demanding curriculum. The cafeteria at the FBI Academy was fantastic, definitely a step up from the food and very basic amenities at FLETC. It even had a Starbucks.

Another big plus was its proximity to Washington, DC. Having the option to get away and explore the city was a nice contrast to being stuck in Glynco, Georgia, where FLETC was located. There was even an FBI Academy bar we frequented called the Boardroom, only accessible to Academy attendees, faculty, and staff, which added to the sense of being in a more relaxed, graduate school-like environment. The FBI Academy felt more like higher education, while FLETC was very much like a military base.

Aside from the major obvious differences between the academies, day-to-day life at the FBI Academy was nothing like what I had experienced previously.

From the start, they reminded us how selective the hiring process was, telling us that for every chair we occupied in the classroom, there were thousands of applicants who didn't make the cut. We were the cream of the crop, and they treated us accordingly, with a level of respect that reflected the prestige of the position.

While the environment had the intensity of cutthroat academics and rigorous physical training, there was also an understanding that the Bureau had already invested heavily in us. They had chosen us for a reason and wanted us to succeed. It wasn't about weeding people out anymore; it was about building us up to meet the high standards of the FBI.

Even some of the skills taught were different from what I had previously learned at FLETC. For example, defensive driving training for the Border Patrol taught a hands-crossed technique; the FBI taught a shuffle steering method, emphasizing the importance of maintaining control of the vehicle at all times.

Classes were also structured very differently from the previous academies I attended.

At the FBI Academy, our days felt like a college schedule, with a focus on law enforcement skills that would shape our careers. The curriculum covered diverse classes, constitutional law, firearms training, defense tactics, physical training, practical exercises, and interviewing techniques, each designed to equip us with the knowledge and abilities necessary to excel in our roles as FBI agents.

In our constitutional law class, we explored the intricacies of searches and seizures, civil rights, and the specific laws and crime types the FBI is tasked with enforcing (like white-collar crime and transnational organized crime). Through rigorous study and immersive discussions, we learned to analyze situations critically and discern the appropriate course of action within the bounds of the law.

Firearms training began with the fundamentals of gun safety and maintenance before we progressed to the firing range. Once we did, we spent countless hours honing our marksmanship skills. (Everyone in the FBI takes quarterly firearms tests to ensure their proficiency remains sharp throughout their career.)

Defensive tactics classes taught us the art of physical control, mastering techniques such as handcuffing, holds, and pressure points. Through hands-on training in arm locks and guards, as well as instruction in boxing, jiu jitsu, and ground fighting, we developed the ability to incapacitate suspects safely and effectively.

Physical training was a daily regimen aimed at ensuring our readiness for the demands of the job. From push-ups and sit-ups to chin-ups and shuttle runs, we pushed our bodies to the limit to meet the stringent standards set forth by the academy.

Practical exercises brought our training to life, simulating real-world scenarios in environments like Hogan's Alley, a mock town designed to replicate the challenges of law enforcement. Working in teams of between four and eight New Agent Trainees (NATs) to replicate a search or arrest team, we faced scenarios ranging from vehicle stops to bank robberies, where we applied our skills to apprehend suspects and gather evidence.

Interview techniques were another essential aspect of our training; role-playing exercises taught us to extract information from suspects *and* witnesses. Learning the FBI's nuanced approach to interrogation, we discovered the delicate balance between persuasion and coercion. We also were shown how to employ tactics such as the "carrot versus the stick" method to elicit crucial information.

When trying to gain cooperation, it's all about understanding the other person's motivation. Some individuals are patriots, driven by a love for their country and a desire to do their civic duty. Others may be looking to work off potential charges or reduce their jail time. Then, of course, there are those motivated by financial incentives. The key is knowing where to push and what motivates them. Once you figure that out, you can tailor your approach to get the cooperation you need.

Throughout our time at the academy, we also used our skills to investigate a real-life case from start to finish. Our class's case involved a bombing plot by a white supremacy gang. At the end of our training, we made the arrest. We were finally ready for graduation and to get started in our careers in the FBI.

Mexican Organized Crime and Drug Squad

In November of 1999, my wife and I relocated to San Francisco for my first assignment as an FBI Agent. My initial assignment placed me in the Mexican Organized Crime and Drug Squad, where I would remain for two years. I assumed that this assignment was an outgrowth of my experience with the Border Patrol and the fact that I had a decent level of Spanish fluency at the time.

It was during the dot-com boom, a time of frenetic energy and boundless opportunity. This was exciting on some fronts, but the cost of living increase had a significant impact on team morale. While the pay wasn't terrible, the starting salary was relatively low, and with the skyrocketing cost of living in the Bay Area at the time, it created an underlying sense of frustration. Every day, we were doing a job we believed was important, yet we watched college kids and recent grads start companies that produced nothing, sold nothing, and still made millions.

It was hard not to feel a little discouraged. A few agents ended up quitting and trying to relocate back to their hometowns, as living in the Bay Area had become nearly unaffordable.

But my wife and I had the benefit of each having a good income without kids at home. (She with the DEA and me the FBI.) We were DINKS: dual income, no kids. We also could rely on family back home if things got difficult. And we rented a very small apartment. It was tough, but we made it work.

It was easier to ignore the quality of life in San Francisco when I was busy at work. While I was relatively inexperienced, I was eager to immerse myself in my new role.

On my first day, I wore a crisply pressed suit, like I was told. Almost everyone else in the FBI wore a suit every day.

I thought I looked great. My Supervisory Special Agent (SSA) didn't.

"If you ever wear that suit again, I'll fucking kill you," he said.

I learned quickly that formal attire had no place in the

gritty world of drug enforcement, even in the FBI. It was jeans and a shirt. That was the dress code for the drug world. A suit was the same as wearing a neon sign that said "federal agent." Over the years, the dress code did change, with suits being required, even for some drug squads. But in 1999, a suit was a no-no.

For the first six months, I absorbed as much job knowledge as I could. Like any newcomer, I found myself saddled with the less glamorous tasks. From conducting surveillance in the dead of night to navigating the labyrinthine streets of the city, I embraced every opportunity to learn.

We used wiretaps to allow us to eavesdrop on conversations conducted in Spanish so we could gather vital intelligence. Working in tandem with linguists, I became a cog in the wheel of a big operation, where multiple agencies (the FBI, DEA, and the San Francisco police department) collaborated to bring down massive criminal enterprises. We orchestrated simultaneous takedowns and executed search warrants. Every action was a piece of a larger puzzle in the fight against organized crime.

9/11 and Hani Hanjour

September 11, 2001 forever changed law enforcement, including the FBI. The terrorist event thrust every FBI office into the forefront of the monumental investigation that followed; it was all any of us focused on for years.

A few of the agents in the San Francisco office were assigned to learn everything they could about Hani Hanjour, the Saudi Arabian hijacker who flew American Airlines Flight 77 into the Pentagon. I was one of them. We traced his footsteps from the moment he set foot in the Bay Area to the moment he died in the attack on the Department of Defense headquarters. Our task was clear: we had to know everything he did—every interaction, every move. Every lead, no matter how trivial, demanded thorough investigation.

The rest of the office was inundated, handling complaints, addressing new terror threats, gathering fresh intelligence, safeguarding the civil rights of the Islamic community, and managing the backlog of hundreds of non-terror-related cases.

Looking back, we were all running on autopilot, completely numb to the exhaustion. I remember not going home for entire weeks at times, either catching a few hours of sleep at the office or just heading home long enough to grab a quick nap, take a shower, and change clothes. The leads we were getting were all over the place. They ranged from people claiming they saw Osama bin Laden pumping gas at a local station to taxi drivers being reported just for being Arab and making negative remarks about the US.

At the same time, we were also dealing with the need to protect the Arab and Muslim communities, who were facing a surge in threats. It was a constant balancing act in the middle of a powder keg of issues, all while a new threat of an imminent attack seemed to pop up every day.

But as months passed and leads dwindled, the reality began to sink in: Hanjour had operated under the radar, leaving no discernible trace of his intentions. Despite exhaustive efforts, there were no red flags, no warning signs. He was a seemingly ordinary man who had seamlessly blended in.

For those of us who worked on the Hanjour case, it was a sobering realization. At the time, 9/11 felt like something that couldn't have been prevented. In the aftermath, many books, reports, and experts have suggested otherwise, if there had been better communication between the CIA and FBI or more effective airport intelligence.

But from my perspective, just weeks or months after the event, and knowing only the limited details from my involvement, it seemed impossible we would have been able to identify this terrorist living among us.

One important distinction that always needs to be made is between the FBI and the CIA (I could write an entire chapter on this, maybe even a whole book, but here's the basic breakdown). The FBI is an investigative agency with arrest powers. While our mission has evolved over the years to include more intelligence work, at its core, the FBI is still a law enforcement organization.

The CIA, on the other hand, is and always has been an intelligence agency. They don't have arrest authority, and their involvement with law enforcement is far more limited. That said, their intelligence work often supports the FBI's investigations and vice versa.

Things get more complicated overseas. While the line between law enforcement and intelligence is pretty clear inside the US, that line tends to blur internationally. In some countries, law enforcement agencies handle intelligence gathering, and intelligence agencies are granted law enforcement powers. In those cases, both the FBI and CIA may end up working with the same foreign partners. That overlap makes coordination and a strong working relationship between the two agencies essential.

White-Collar Crime Squad

After 9/11, resources were poured into counterterrorism efforts, and the landscape of law enforcement shifted dramatically. The FBI transformed from a law enforcement agency to an intelligence powerhouse.

As the counterterrorism dust settled and the urgency behind those efforts subsided, I went back to the drug squad. As soon as I returned to my old squad, I decided I wanted a change of pace, so I took an opportunity to join the white-collar crime squad.

But I knew from the outset that it wouldn't be a long-term commitment for me. I had entered a meticulous world of number crunching and paper trails, a far cry from the adrenaline-fueled pursuits of drug and terrorism investigations.

Even amid the mountains of financial documents and corporate filings, though, the cases we pursued held their own intrigue, like one that arose from the aftermath of the Enron scandal: the California energy crisis.

The California energy crisis occurred in the early 2000s, primarily around 2000–2001. It was a period marked by rolling blackouts, soaring electricity prices, and instability in the state's power supply. At the heart of the issue was Enron, a major energy company that later became infamous for its role in corporate fraud.

Enron, based in Houston, Texas, started as a natural gas company but grew into a significant player in the energy trading and commodities market. The company was known for its innovative financial strategies, but behind the scenes, it engaged in questionable practices that ultimately led to its downfall.

In the case of the California energy crisis, Enron, along with a handful of other energy companies, was involved in market manipulation. After the state deregulated its energy market, allowing companies to compete in selling electricity, a few players in the energy market took advantage of the system. The companies were able to artificially create energy shortages, which drove up prices. By restricting the flow of energy, they sold electricity at much higher rates during times of increased demand.

This manipulation had a significant impact on California's economy and contributed to the energy crisis. The fraud that was found in the California energy markets came to light as part of broader investigations into the company's practices, leading to its bankruptcy in 2001. Many of its executives were later convicted of fraud. The situation highlighted the risks of deregulated markets and the importance of oversight in preventing market abuse.

After interviewing individuals implicated in the fraud, we uncovered a web of deception that touched every level of the organization. The manipulation of energy markets had resulted in rolling blackouts across California. Energy companies had reaped massive profits at the expense of the public.

By listening in on industry-recorded conversations and conducting surveillance, we pieced it all together and made arrests. One trader, faced with the prospect of jail time, revealed the inner workings of what they termed the "Death Star strategy." This involved deliberately manipulating the California power grid. Specifically, the traders made it look like parts of California were overloaded with electricity, causing "congestion." This resulted in a need to route energy in a more costly way, which increased the energy company's profits.

But the traders who undertook these fraudulent tactics got caught, destroying trust and damaging reputations in the long run.

"At what point did you know it was illegal?" we asked.

"Right now," the trader said.

This answer spoke volumes about a culture of corporate greed. For those involved, the focus had always been on maximizing profits, with little regard for the consequences of their actions. So much so, they were unaware they were breaking the law.

At the end of the day, we were not merely prosecuting crimes; we were shining a light on systemic flaws and holding accountable those responsible.

Muay Thai boxing

It was around this time when Thailand made its first appearance in my life. My wife and I had purchased a condo in San Francisco. Shortly after moving, I was looking for a place to exercise near the condo, and a quick internet search led me to a gym with a name I had never heard before: Muay Thai. I decided to give it a try. It wasn't until I walked into the gym for the first class that I learned Muay Thai was kickboxing, and the "Thai" in the name meant Thailand. I loved the class, and I was so intrigued by Thai culture. Over the next few months, I became more and more fascinated by the idea of visiting Thailand. The Muay Thai instructors convinced me, and I booked a trip for my wife and me to visit Bangkok and Phuket. The trip was nothing short of amazing. The food, people, energy, culture…everything.

And the magic of Thailand took hold. I was sold on Thailand from the first time I stepped foot in the country.

By 2003, I decided to pursue opportunities abroad, specifically in Thailand. So I reached out to the legat assigned there.

"I'm eager to explore the possibility of becoming Legat Bangkok," I wrote in an email. "What should I do?"

He advised me to find a role in a terrorism or Asian organized crime squad, get a temporary overseas assignment, and take Thai language courses.

The first thing I did was take the role of supervisor for the Asian organized crime squad in San Francisco. I oversaw a team of 14 agents. It was a challenging yet rewarding experience, as we tackled cases ranging from drug rings to human trafficking, mostly within the Chinatown community.

Not too long after I started in my new role, I began taking Thai language classes at the local Thai Buddhist temple. And in 2006, I took a monthlong assignment in Bangkok as the ALAT, where I was tasked with addressing a backlog of cases and forging connections within the local community.

During this assignment, I hit the ground running. I familiarized myself with embassy protocols and established crucial contacts within the region. I worked alongside the Assistant United States Attorney; heads of other US federal law enforcement agencies such as the Secret Service, Homeland Security, and DEA, along with intelligence agencies like the CIA and NSA; and representatives from countless other agencies.

On top of that, there were police attachés from countries like Australia, Germany, Japan, and England, just to name a few. And then, of course, there were the Thai police, with officers assigned to every kind of crime you could imagine. I made it a point to connect with as many of them as possible. It was a huge network of people, all working toward the same goal, and it made the job even more dynamic.

I fell in love with the job almost immediately. Within a few days, I knew this was what I wanted to do for as long as possible. I remember calling my wife and telling her, "When I finish this assignment, I want to be the full-time ALAT, then head back to HQ for a quick stint, and finish my career as Legat Bangkok."

And that was exactly what I set out to do. I needed a bit of luck along the way, but I made it clear to anyone who asked that I had found my calling in the FBI, and I was all in.

I loved everything about it: the fast-paced nature of the job, learning the language and culture, navigating the complexities of the Thai bureaucracy. It all fascinated me. I was genuinely excited to go to work every single day. I'd start at 7:00 a.m. and wouldn't stop until late at night, and I loved every minute of it.

One aspect of the legat job that rarely gets talked about, even among legats themselves, is just how dramatically different your work life becomes when you're stationed overseas versus when you're working stateside. When I first started my assignment in Thailand, I couldn't have imagined the kinds of meetings I'd be part of, the powerful people I'd speak with on a regular basis, or the level of decision-making I'd be responsible for, often with little to no oversight.

I was the FBI's representative in Thailand. That meant I met with the US Ambassador, sometimes daily. I met with the Chief of Police for the Royal Thai Police, the Attorney General of Thailand, and business executives across all sectors. In many of these meetings, I was either requesting assistance or fielding requests from others. When I spoke, it wasn't just me talking: it was the FBI. My words were often taken as gospel. My opinions, suggestions, and sign-off on certain initiatives were perceived as the Bureau's official stance.

I have countless examples of being asked what I thought

about a particular issue and then watching my words turn into action. Whether it was providing feedback on arrest procedures or weighing in on the creation of a Joint Terrorism Task Force, I found myself in the thick of high-level decisions. And I take great pride in the fact that I was able to not only hold my own in those moments but thrive.

Fast-forward to the end of my first tour as Assistant Legal Attaché. I transitioned back to FBI Headquarters in Washington, DC, where I was assigned to the International Operations Division (IOD), the team that oversees all legat offices. My goal was to stay at HQ just long enough to get back overseas and finish out my career as a legat.

My time in DC was...educational. While many agents spend time at HQ before they're ever assigned abroad, I went straight from San Francisco to Bangkok, so this was my first real taste of HQ life. On day one, I sat in on a meeting about a situation in one of our Asia-Pacific offices. The discussion centered on how to handle a sensitive FBI matter with other law enforcement leadership in the embassy. I had only been in the job for a single day, but I was also the only person in the room who had actually worked overseas.

So I offered my input. Honestly, it wasn't a tough call. I'd handled far more delicate matters in Thailand. I explained how I would have approached it. The response? Something along the lines of "That might make sense, but we need to get approval from at least two levels of supervisors before we move forward."

I was stunned. I had made that exact kind of decision many times without ever needing anyone's permission. And this wasn't even a high-stakes issue by comparison. That moment made something very clear: most people at FBIHQ had no idea how complex, high-profile, and sensitive the decisions were that I'd been making every day in Thailand, with zero requirement to "get a supervisor's approval."

I missed Bangkok immediately. And I appreciated the legat role even more than I already had.

After my short stint as acting ALAT, I returned to the United States in December of 2006 and waited for the opportunity to return to Thailand permanently. I had built a strong rapport with the ALAT, and in mid-2007, when there was an opening for the next ALAT position in Bangkok, that connection, and being a reputable, known entity, helped to get my name on the short list of candidates. When the FBI made its selection, he weighed in and fought to get my name to the top of the list.

And I got selected as ALAT Bangkok.

CHAPTER 3

WHERE AM I?

ON SEPTEMBER 27, 2019, AT A FIVE-STAR HOTEL ON the outskirts of Bangkok, I witnessed one of my closest friends, Jaturong "Aod" Thongphunlordkul, a Royal Thai Police officer, marry the love of his life.

It was a massive Thai wedding. Hundreds of people were in attendance, and the event was spectacular.

The wedding was a grand affair: men in suits, held indoors in a large banquet hall, with room for hundreds of guests. I had the honor of giving the best man speech, and I delivered it in both Thai and English, which turned out to be the highlight of the night. People who only knew me as Aod's FBI colleague were genuinely surprised to see how close we were, while those who had met me before were stunned at how well I spoke Thai. It was a moment that brought everyone together, and the reaction made it all the more memorable. Aod and I first met out of necessity, he was a RTP Foreign Affairs officer with a portfolio that included the FBI, and we hit it off immediately. The reason was simple: we shared the same approach to police work. We never took no for an answer and tackled each problem step by step, keeping things steady without too many ups and downs. Over the years, he was transferred to different departments, and my first tour in Bangkok ended. Life kept moving, but we always stayed close.

I helped Aod by making sure others noticed his value. The fact that the Head of the FBI in Thailand saw him as an indispensable resource meant higher-ranking officers in the RTP started paying attention to him, and he was always grateful for that. In turn, he helped me navigate the complexities of the RTP bureaucracy, guiding me through the puzzle of Thai formalities and even assisting me with the language. From navigating tricky situations like Thai funerals to understanding the ins and outs of the culture, Aod was my go-to.

We're still close friends today, and we continue to help each other whenever we can.

I have made a home in Thailand, and I have retired here. My family and best friends are here. There is no reason to leave.

I fell in love with Thailand when I first visited in 2002. And until I moved there permanently in 2008, it was all I talked about, all I cared about. My interest in the country, its culture, and its people cannot be overstated. From the moment the plane first touched down, I knew I wanted to be in Thailand.

And not just to visit. I wanted to *live* there.

My entire life, I had lived in a lot of different places: I grew up in Maryland, went to college in Upstate New York, and worked as a Border Patrol Agent in Southern Arizona, a Department of Commerce agent in Chicago, and an FBI agent in San Francisco.

Thailand was the only place that truly felt like home.

My wife loved it, too, and was on board with pursuing moving to Thailand full time, so I changed my career path within the FBI to pursue a career as Legat Bangkok.

(As Legat Bangkok, I was also responsible for coverage of Laos and Myanmar. I'll share an interesting story from my time there as well.)

Bangkok or bust

Bangkok is hot. Anyone who's spent time in the city knows this. But for those who haven't had the pleasure of visiting the most-visited city in the world, let me give you some context.

It regularly tops rankings as the hottest major city on Earth, yet somehow, people still underestimate what that means. When I first planned a vacation to Thailand, a friend told me, "Turn on your oven, wait for it to heat up, then stick your face inside." That, he said, is what Bangkok feels like for nine months of the year.

He couldn't have been more spot-on.

All day and night, it's hot. Even after the sun goes down, the heat lingers. By the time the city wakes up enough for its infamous traffic to kick in, the sun is already locked in for the day. You get used to taking two (or more) showers and going through at least two outfits. From March through October, the heat is so relentless that by November, when the temperature drops even slightly, you catch yourself saying it's "cool" outside.

I've learned to savor the rare days when I actually consider wearing a sweatshirt. And seeing Thais bundled up in winter hats and down jackets when it's in the 70s (low 20s Celsius) is always a fun sight.

Even the air smells hot. But Bangkok's air has a distinct scent, too, something I've never been able to put my finger on but always love. One of the best feelings is walking out of Suvarnabhumi Airport: you step from the crisp, air-conditioned terminal into the heavy warmth outside, and the scent of Bangkok hits you. It's hard to describe, but once you've felt and smelled the air in Thailand, you never forget it.

Sweating becomes second nature. It happens all the time. Daily decisions—what to wear, where to eat, how to get there—all start factoring in the likelihood of sweat. Air-conditioning takes on a sacred role in daily life. The malls, the BTS Skytrain, the metro, even a quick trip into a 7-Eleven becomes a mini vacation from the heat.

And when you leave Thailand and travel somewhere with what most people would consider "normal" temperatures, you'll find yourself cold when everyone else is hot.

When my wife and I arrived in Thailand, with our (at the time) two-year-old son, we knew we wanted to live in downtown Bangkok.

This was atypical.

When we first came to Thailand, most American Embassy personnel lived outside Bangkok, close to the International School of Bangkok, in a town that closely resembled a street from a scene in *Desperate Housewives*. It was very Americanized.

That didn't interest my wife or me in the slightest. We wanted to live in the hustle and bustle of downtown. So we were assigned diplomatic housing in the middle of Bangkok. We both worked (my wife was an Intelligence Analyst with the DEA at the time), so we hired a nanny (who was also a maid) to help out.

The life of a diplomat is awesome. We were coming from San Francisco during the dot-com era, and we were government workers. We were middle class in San Francisco. In Bangkok, we lived the life of diplomats: we had money to try the best restaurants, and we traveled extensively throughout Thailand and the region, which was an incredible experience.

On top of that, we were able to save a lot. It's one of the main reasons I was able to retire at 48 and have the option not to work again, though I chose to continue working on my own terms.

A first-class lifestyle at a third-world price

There is nothing better than being an American...except being an American overseas. In Thailand, we lived a first-class lifestyle at a third-world price.

Why Bangkok? It's a city that strikes a unique balance. You've got cheaper cities that don't offer much in terms of quality of life, and then you've got more expensive cities that are out of reach. Bangkok is both affordable and dynamic. Sure, it comes with the chaos, the occasional rat, and the unpredictability you find in many developing countries. But at the same time, you can afford experiences you may not be able to elsewhere, so you get the best of both worlds.

Bangkok has an edge to it, and some people don't like that. But for adventure junkies like my wife and me, it was perfect. We wanted the excitement and unpredictability, but we also wanted access to the comforts of a nice restaurant or a luxury stay. Plus, the cost of living is fantastic, making it an easy choice for us.

We loved the lifestyle, but we also admired the amazing people and the incredible food and culture.

Most people have at least tried or seen Thai food, but for those who haven't truly experienced it, the magic lies in the combination of salty, sweet, sour, and spicy flavors. That balance is what makes Thai food so special, and in my opinion, it really is the greatest food in the world. The regional cuisine from Northeastern Thailand, known as Isaan food, is the best of the best: bold, flavorful, and unforgettable.

After you get used to those intense flavors, American food just seems so bland by comparison. It lacks the same explosion of tastes that Thai food delivers. On top of that, the availability of amazing, cheap street food and fresh exotic fruits only adds to the allure. It's hard to beat that kind of culinary experience.

The weather, although it can get too hot sometimes, is still great, and the people are even better. Thailand is known as "The Land of Smiles," and Thai people really embody that every day.

I'm not saying people aren't nice in those other cities. What I'm getting at is when people ask, "Aren't there 'nicer' cities?" they're usually thinking of big, famous places like New York, London, or Paris. Sure, those cities are out there, but they're expensive, and they don't have the same excitement and edge that Bangkok does. On the flip side, are there cheaper cities? Definitely. Places like Jakarta and Manila, but they don't offer the lifestyle you can have in Bangkok. It really gives you the best of both worlds: affordability and excitement.

But what I love most is the contrast. One day, you could be navigating floods or political unrest, and the next, you're dining in Michelin-starred restaurants, attending world-class concerts, and shopping in malls that outshine anything in the US. The mix of adventure and value is what makes living in Thailand so special.

And I had the best job in the world: I got to work as an FBI agent in a foreign country...and I was able to do *active* police work. Legats in other countries were mostly paper pushers, where the actual police work was only handled by local law enforcement agencies.

In many legat offices, like London, Ottawa, or Canberra, much of the FBI's work involves providing information or official requests to the local police. Those agencies then handle the investigation on their own, gather the necessary information, and send a response back to the FBI in a timely manner. From there, the FBI agent writes up the response and sends it to the requesting agent in the US.

In Thailand, though, it was a different story. I had the opportunity to be much more hands-on. I conducted interviews, assisted in executing search warrants, and even joined the team going out to track down fugitives. I could personally go to banks to request documents or be involved in the day-to-day work of an FBI agent, just like I would in the US.

What *wasn't* similar to the US was the way I was treated in Thailand. They looked at me like I was Batman. Their sole experience with the FBI was what they had seen on TV or read in books. To them, FBI agents were like superheroes.

It was cool to be admired and looked up to, but it was also a lot of pressure. How could I let them down?

Of course, I was always working alongside the Royal Thai Police, as they had the actual enforcement authority. I didn't have any law enforcement powers outside the US without their assistance, but the collaboration allowed me to be directly involved in the work in ways that aren't as common in other countries.

A time of political unrest

Was everything about Thailand amazing?

No. A tough part of the transition to Bangkok was seeing the city's extreme poverty. The level of impoverishment here can go beyond anything you typically see in the US, and that's hard to witness sometimes.

Being so far from family was difficult, especially around the holidays or when someone back home was sick or needed my wife or me. It could make the distance feel much greater.

It's always hot in Thailand, and sometimes it's *very* hot. I hate snow, so I'll take the heat any day, but April can be unbearable.

Lesser hardships, but still big changes for us, were that we had to drive on the other side of the road, and my wife had to learn Thai. (My Thai was already pretty good, because of my devotion to studying Thai during my time in San Francisco and my previous time in Thailand.) Then there's the rainy season: flooded streets are a regular occurrence, and that gets old pretty fast. Bangkok's traffic is another issue; you can easily spend hours stuck in one spot.

We also arrived during a time of political unrest. There were two warring factions (each side wanted power), resulting in protests and a successful coup. The military took over and didn't relinquish power for years. Protesters had even gone so far as to cause the largest international airport in Thailand to have to cease operations. In fact, the airport was opened only a few weeks before we moved.

The two sides were distinguished by the shirt color they wore. The red-shirts began as supporters of former Prime Minister Thaksin Shinawatra, who was ousted by a military coup in September of 2006. Their support later shifted to Thailand's ruling Pheu Thai Party, led by Thaksin's sister, Yingluck Shinawatra. However, back in 2008, their loyalty was fully behind Thaksin himself.

On the other side were the yellow-shirts, who opposed Thaksin and were instrumental in the street protests that eventually led to the 2006 coup. The red shirts, formally known as the United Front for Democracy Against Dictatorship (UDD), mainly consisted of rural workers from outside Bangkok, but also included students, left-wing activists, and some businesspeople. They viewed the urban and military elite's influence on Thai politics as a threat to democracy.

The yellow shirts, like the reds, were initially united by their opposition to Thaksin. Known as the People's Alliance for Democracy (PAD), they were a loose group of royalists, ultranationalists, and the urban middle class. They were the driving force behind the protests that culminated in the 2006 military coup.

Thai politics have always been a bit…unpredictable. One minute someone's leading the country, and the next minute they're ousted, in exile, back in power, or suddenly the subject of a no-confidence vote. Leadership changes fast—sometimes through elections, sometimes through backroom deals, and sometimes through full-blown coups.

Thaksin Shinawatra, a former Prime Minister, was ousted and spent years in exile, only to later return. Five years later, his sister became Prime Minister and was also removed from office during mass political unrest. Ten years after Yingluk was named Prime Minister, Thaksin's daughter, Paetongtarn Shinawatra, rose to lead the country herself.

That's the thing: Thai politics operate on their own rhythm. The Prime Minister isn't directly elected by the people but chosen by whichever party or coalition of parties holds the most seats in Parliament. That means power can shift in unexpected ways, and alliances can change overnight.

For many Thai citizens, political instability, including military coups, has become part of the landscape. While not ideal, it's often seen as one of several possible outcomes when governments lose favor or legitimacy. And while each chapter of political drama is unique, the constant is change.

So if you're reading this and wondering what happened next, there's a good chance it already did.

The FBI and a Thai coup

The FBI works with whoever is in power because our job is law enforcement, not politics. The US government is against coups, though, so when it quickly classified the Thai military action as a coup, a review of US aid to Thailand was triggered. Under federal laws that prohibit American assistance to countries where democratic governments have been overthrown, at least $10M in US funding was at risk of being withdrawn. In a statement, then–Secretary of State John Kerry emphasized the potential consequences:[2]

> While we value our long friendship with the Thai people, this act will have negative implications for the US–Thai relationship, especially for our relationship with the Thai military. We are reviewing our military and other assistance and engagements, consistent with US law.

The move signaled a shift in the historically strong US–Thai relations, particularly in terms of military cooperation.

I was told to stand down until the US figured out how to relate to the new government.

The suspension of US aid to Thailand wasn't about pay or benefits and didn't directly affect anything beyond government-level assistance. In reality, it was a temporary measure that lasted only a few months. The US government quickly realized that cutting aid was counterproductive to broader efforts, so steps were taken to minimize the negative impact. The focus shifted to ensuring that the relationship,

---

2   John Kerry, "Statement by Secretary Kerry: Coup in Thailand" (press statement, US Department of State, May 22, 2014), https://2009-2017.state.gov/secretary/remarks/2014/05/226446.htm.

especially in areas like cooperation and security, remained as strong as possible while navigating the legal restrictions.

There is one political protest in particular that stands out. Protestors had burned down part of a mall. It was at a major intersection in downtown Bangkok and was the largest gathering of Thai protesters in Thai history.

This was in 2010, and the political landscape was still tense. Despite Thaksin's removal, the red shirts managed to keep their coalition intact, maintaining control of the political arena for a while. However, the yellow shirts, aligned with the more conservative elements of Thai society, kept finding ways to disqualify political parties or candidates for Prime Minister. Eventually, this allowed the yellow shirt-aligned Democrats to take over the coalition and appoint a Prime Minister of their own. The red shirts viewed this maneuver as a "silent coup," believing it was an underhanded way to wrest power without a direct military intervention.

My wife and I lived downtown, and during all this, we were asked to shelter in place (in our home) in case protestors entered the building and vandalized it...or worse. Maybe they were coming for expats.

That wasn't the only time of political unrest in Thailand while I served as a legat. In 2014, two political parties were at odds, sparking more major protests. In the new wave of protests, entire intersections on some of the busiest streets in the capital were closed, causing chaos for months. The yellow shirts represented business and the royal family, and the red shirts were worn by people of the populist movement.

Politics were so intense during that time that I couldn't wear gear representing my favorite ice hockey team, the Washington Capitals, for years because everything I owned for the team was solid red.

Thailand gets in your blood

Thailand gets in your blood. When I first visited, I knew within a week that I wanted to move there.

When I finally did in 2008, as ALAT Bangkok, I hit the ground running, personally and professionally. I had made friends during my monthlong temporary assignment, so I reconnected with them. I had made connections within the Royal Thai Police at that time, too, which I rekindled as well.

I also reconnected with my new boss. I had known him for a couple of years: we had stayed in touch after my temporary assignment there, when I covered 100 leads during the month I was there.

But there were a lot of people I didn't know, too, so my first goal was to meet everyone. I went from office to office to learn who was in charge of each department: fugitives, white-collar crime, and terrorism, for example. I wanted to meet them all.

This is the thing about policing in Asia; most of the work gets done between 8:00 and 10:00 p.m., when everyone is out eating and drinking. In Thailand specifically, the FBI name goes a long way, but I learned early on that socializing over a meal and some drinks is a legat's number-one skill.

Whiskey soda, anyone?

Drinking-wise, I had always been able to hold my own. My dad was a big drinker, and I was in a fraternity in college and played hockey all my life (most hockey players drink). I also drank socially all throughout my time with the Border Patrol, US Department of Commerce, and FBI, state-side.

Social drinking had always been a part of my life, but

nothing prepared me for the social-drinking skills of the RTP.

The first time I got drunk with my RTP friends it was a Monday or a Tuesday, a school night, which is typical. In the Asian business world, weekends are for family time, so that leaves the weekdays for drinking and socializing with friends and colleagues.

I stumbled home around 2:00 a.m. on Monday and was at my desk at 7:00 a.m. on Tuesday, ready for the formal US Embassy weekly country team meeting. I sat in the back of the room among all of my American colleagues, including the US Ambassador, and did my best to pretend I wasn't as hungover as I actually was.

As it turned out, it was just another day on the job.

Over time, I learned how to balance my late nights with my early mornings. It took a few months, but it was soon known that "Khun John" (me) would never say no to a whiskey soda, the RTP's drink of choice, on a Tuesday.

I was able to integrate myself with the RTP quickly because I knew going in that most of the work happened over whiskey sodas, after 8:00 p.m. I was prepared, so making friends and earning their trust happened almost immediately.

Almost everything we did socially paved the way for work-related needs. On a broad scale, we were going out all the time. Now, I wasn't going out with the same group every time. I made it a point to build good relationships with multiple departments. So what might have been a monthly outing for one group turned into a weekly thing for me, as I rotated between different teams.

It wasn't unusual that if I needed to ask a high-level General for something in a Thursday morning meeting, I'd be out having drinks with his subordinates the night before. In Thai military and police circles, it's common for decisions to be made and briefed informally before the actual meeting. The official meeting itself often ended up being just a formality for the topic we had already discussed over drinks.

Over drinks was also how I bonded with Aod. We became the closest of friends–not just work colleagues but a friendship forged over many long nights of Sangsom (a Thai rum that is one of my drinks of choice when having a night out) and soda.

Building relationships

I went everywhere with my boss when I first started, but I didn't need as much handholding because I had already worked temporarily in Thailand before. I spoke Thai and had studied the culture, food, and music. I'd even spent time going to the local Thai temple.

My boss trusted me with leads right from the start, giving me info for contacts I hadn't met yet. The handholding mostly happened within the embassy, where I had to meet the internal agency folks. It was 2008, and the majority of them were new, not the same people I worked with when I was there in 2006.

When it came to building relationships *outside* the embassy, the Thai police were a huge help. I'd ask them, and they'd call their friends to introduce me. I was also able to rekindle old relationships established from my first assignment and set up meetings as soon as I moved back. I reconnected with colleagues I'd met before, and they introduced me to even more people.

It didn't take long to build a huge contact list.

One of my key partners was Aod. Some foreign police work closely with the RTP's Foreign Affairs Division, the division Aod called home, and while that's a typical route, I also wanted to branch out and work with as many good cops as I could. I found key officers in many of the RTP's departments to work with, depending on the case. At the same time, Aod remained my closest contact in the police. Even if I planned to work with an officer in a specific department, I tried to bring Aod into the investigation in some capacity. I wasn't always able to do this, but I always tried. He had the same mindset as I did when it came to police work, and he backed up my decisions. We'd work terrorism cases, track fugitives, and travel many times throughout the country in the furtherance of investigations. Anything I needed to do, he was right there with me.

Aod was also great at getting people to say yes when I couldn't. I'd often ask him, "Aod, is this a hard no, or can we get it to a yes?" He always knew the right moves, the steps to take to turn a no into a yes. He would lay it out for me, "Do this, this, and this," and it usually worked. He always told me the truth, which is one of the many reasons we became close friends and why I gave the best-man speech at his wedding.

Thailand isn't just a place; its culture is strong enough that you adapt to its way of life. From the moment I arrived in 2008, I knew this was where I wanted to be. The culture, the people, the food, and even the chaos all made sense to me. I quickly integrated into the professional and social circles that defined my work as Legat Bangkok, building relationships and trust with the RTP and other law enforcement agencies. I feel a good part of my success stemmed from my understanding and acceptance of cultural cues. Knowing I wanted to make Thailand my home, not just a pit stop in my career, gave me the motivation to start trying to acclimate more into Thai society. I wanted to show my colleagues and friends I understood the culture and acted accordingly. I also focused on making personal connections, like my friendship with Aod, because they are just as important as professional ones.

Thailand's unique blend of excitement and comfort made it the perfect place for my family and me. The opportunities for real police work, not just paperwork, kept me on my toes and gave me a level of fulfillment I hadn't experienced in other roles. I was lucky to not only experience the adventure of living in a city as dynamic as Bangkok but also to establish a life here. It's why, after everything, I chose to retire in Thailand, a country that got under my skin and into my heart. It's more than just a place to live; it's home.

CHAPTER 4

THE DEATH OF DAVID CARRADINE

IN JUNE OF 2009, JUST SIX MONTHS INTO MY TIME AS ALAT, I was involved in what turned out to be the most high-profile case of my FBI career: the death of actor David Carradine.

David Carradine of *Kill Bill* fame was in Bangkok to shoot a low-budget movie. He was found dead in Bangkok on June 4, 2009, in a part of the city I knew well. It was across the street from a club called the Pent (known for its beautiful hostesses), which the RTP and I had frequented for a whiskey soda or two.

Oddly enough, I didn't first hear about Carradine's death from the RTP. I heard it from friends and family members back in the US. It was breaking news there.

"David Carradine Found Dead in Thailand" was the headline. In the early stages, some news outlets speculated about the cause of death, while others stuck to reporting how he was found, avoiding any conjecture.

In the first 24 hours following the incident, no photos emerged, fueling rumors about the cause of death. Speculation among the family about possible scenarios like robbery or murder intensified due to the vague initial reports.

Some newspapers and websites briefly published leaked photos of Carradine that supported an autoerotic asphyxiation theory (he was found with one end of a rope tied around his neck and the other end, his testicles). The photos were quickly retracted.

When the story hit CNN during a *Larry King Live* segment, the announcement detailed that he was found hanging in a closet, with ropes tied around him.

Why did the FBI call me to help with the case? Two reasons, in my opinion. First, the family specifically requested FBI assistance, and we try to be responsive, especially when someone with the kind of public profile David Carradine had is involved. Second, FBI Director Robert Mueller (yes, *that* Director Mueller) was scheduled to be in LA the following week, and he was set to appear in the "Hollywood community" to present an award to the star of the old FBI TV show. There was a good chance the Hollywood press would ask questions about Carradine, so the Bureau wanted to be prepared.

My family and friends called me because they always reach out when Thailand is in the news. And when a story is big enough to make headlines in the US, they definitely call for the inside scoop. This time, they had heard the FBI was asked to help, so they had even more reason to expect me to have the "untold story."

I knew David Carradine from the old *Kung Fu* TV show, though I didn't watch it much. But *Kill Bill*? I loved those movies, so I was definitely familiar with his work. Plus, the Carradine family name was well known from other films and TV shows, so he wasn't just any celebrity.

When I got the call, my first reaction was purely from the perspective of an FBI agent. I immediately started thinking about how I could help and what steps we needed to take. The personal connection to his movies was secondary. My focus was on the job.

You have to take the emotion out of everything when you're in this line of work. You can't let feelings cloud your judgment. It's about finding that balance, being invested enough to care, to want to help, to train and prepare yourself for these moments. But when it's time to act, you have to keep those emotions in check.

In this case, I wanted to help the Thai police maintain a good reputation, assist the Carradine family in finding answers, and uphold the reputation of the FBI. It was about making sure everything was handled professionally and objectively, without letting personal feelings interfere with the task at hand.

And if the family truly believed he was murdered, it was the FBI's responsibility to give them closure.

Requesting the FBI's help

David Carradine was a celebrity, so it was always likely his death would be high profile. But his death was *especially* high profile because it was taboo; he was hanging naked in his hotel room when he was found. From what I understood, the Royal Thai Police had investigated the scene and determined the cause of death to be autoerotic asphyxiation. Carradine had suffocated himself to enhance his sexual pleasure during climax, and he had died because of it.

But Carradine's family didn't want to hear it. They suspected foul play, so they hired Mark Geragos to represent them. His priority was to protect the Carradine family's reputation and legacy.

Mark Geragos is a famous celebrity attorney. He has represented Michael Jackson, Winona Ryder, Barry Bonds' trainer, Chris Brown, Colin Kaepernick, and Jussie Smollett.

I didn't interact with him directly. The only thing I know is that he was part of the CNN broadcast. I mention him and his involvement to highlight how truly high profile the case was and the pressure I felt to handle it correctly. It wasn't only the publicity surrounding the case itself; there was also the fact that someone like Mark Geragos, who's known for his sharp legal mind, would be watching closely, looking for any gaps in our case or assistance. His presence raised the stakes, and I knew there was no room for error.

The day after David Carradine was found dead, the family, together with Geragos, went on *Larry King Live*. They told the world they suspected foul play and that they had asked the FBI to help investigate the case.

Requesting help from the FBI overseas may seem innocent, but it was a direct insult to the RTP. It was like calling them incompetent. The request, even though they didn't mean it that way, was dismissive and condescending.

Why would you need the help of the FBI if you believed the RTP was doing a good job? Most everyone in the RTP is very patient. But if you question their abilities and tell them they aren't doing a good job, they lose face, which is a big deal in most Asian cultures. It's one of the worst things that can happen.

Losing face akin to this kind of embarrassment is hard to explain. It's a concept we don't really have in America. The best way to understand it? Imagine someone embarrassing you to an unexplainable degree, to the point where it shakes you to your core. The experience has been described as feeling outright intimidated or humiliated in front of onlookers, caused by verbal or nonverbal treatment. And helping friends, family, or colleagues "save face" is a satisfying feeling.

Professionally, it was my job to help the Carradine family investigate his death. Personally, I wanted to do it because I knew the RTP were good police officers and that they were getting a bad reputation. I wanted to help with the case because I wanted to help them.

A steep learning curve

David Carradine was found dead on a Thursday. I heard about it on Friday, when the news broke in the US. On Saturday, I received the call from my boss.

Immediately after I got off the phone with my boss, I contacted Police Colonel Rungrote "Bung" Thakurapunyasiri, the Commander of the Royal Thai Police Lumpinee Station, which covered the area where Carradine's body was found. After I reached out and got him up to speed on my request, I told him Carradine's family had contacted the FBI for help. He jumped on it. He was already knee-deep in the case and wanted to do anything he could to get me what I needed.

Meanwhile, my whole family was settling into life in Thailand. My wife was working for the DEA in the embassy, and my son was making friends. I joined an ice hockey league, where I met an amazing group of people who are still some of my closest friends to this day. Everything was as good as I expected, and the longer I was there, the more I loved it.

But at the office, even though I had spent a month there a couple of years earlier while on temporary assignment, there was a steep learning curve. When David Carradine was found, I had only been working in my position as ALAT for six months, and in that short amount of time, I had been given a temporary assignment to work in the legat office in Jakarta in support of a visit by then-Secretary of State Hillary Clinton. I was there during the planning stage to help prepare for her trip, which meant I had even less time on the ground in Thailand.

When the Carradine case hit, I had to learn a lot...and I had to do it quickly.

A melting pot

The type of work in the Bangkok office of the FBI, much like the city itself, was a mix of everything. Bangkok is a melting pot of nationalities, with every kind of entertainment imaginable, and it's chaotic: 24/7, anything goes. Similarly, during my first six months in the office, we saw cases linked to just about every type of crime: terrorism, white-collar crime, cybercrime, you name it. Unlike other overseas offices that might focus on one or two areas, my experience in Bangkok was diverse.

So while I was getting to know a foreign land, learning the ways of the Royal Thai Police, and navigating the daily grind of working in an embassy, I was also getting a crash course in crime types I hadn't dealt with during my time in San Francisco. It was an intense but invaluable education.

It had been a busy, grueling, and intense half a year, but I was grateful for it because I had made many connections, one of which was Bung. So when my boss asked me to call him, it was easy: I already had his number on my phone.

A delicate dance

Navigating this situation felt like a delicate dance. There was no room for error, and the stakes were high; any misstep could inadvertently implicate the FBI, potentially fueling speculations of foul play. I recognized the importance of articulating the facts accurately, ensuring both the family and the FBI were convinced of the truth.

I felt the weight of expectation; I needed to get this right. It was my first big case in Thailand, and it was important to me that I do well. I was a lot younger than most of my Royal Thai Police counterparts, which didn't help, and the aura and reputation surrounding the Hollywood-portrayed FBI Agent made it even worse; the Royal Thai Police expected me to be brilliant. And then there were the FBI standards to uphold, along with the desire to do justice to everyone involved and earn their approval.

So needless to say, I was stressed.

A key part of the stress of being an FBI agent (especially one working solo with local police who expect you to be Batman) is not letting that stress show on the outside. You have to internalize it, push it down, and keep moving. That's the hallmark of a good agent: no one can tell how stressed you really are.

I had tackled tough, high-profile cases previously, but none had involved scrutinizing my colleagues' integrity. Getting it right was nonnegotiable.

Personally, I used that pressure, fed off it, and let it drive me to get the job done.

The Swissotel

David Carradine's body was found in the Swissotel Nai Lert in downtown Bangkok. When I called Bung, he arranged for me to meet the lead investigator in the hotel lobby the following morning.

On Sunday, I jumped on a motorbike to meet him. When I got there, the hotel was busy, and the lobby was packed.

"I want to know everything," I said as soon as we sat down.

He opened his laptop and showed me at least a hundred photos of the crime scene and Carradine's body. Carradine was covered in tattoos and looked to be about the same age as my dad, which at the time was around 71. (I found out later that Carradine was 72 at the time of his death.)

After reviewing the lobby footage, I took several steps to confirm the details the RTP had gathered, ensuring there was no foul play involved. First, I went through the hotel's CCTV footage for the entire time Mr. Carradine stayed there, and no one entered the room other than Carradine and hotel staff.

One of the allegations made by the family was that "ladyboys," or transgender men, had gone to his room and robbed him. In hotels in Thailand, every male tourist who brings a Thai "lady friend" to his room is required to have the guest sign in. For everyone's safety, the hotel staff is also required to hold onto the guest's ID. I reviewed the hotel's sign-in book and verified that Mr. Carradine had no guests during his stay. Added to this, all his personal belongings, including cash and valuables, were still in his room.

It also looked like he traveled to Thailand with the tools used in the act (more on this next), and money was left in plain sight in the room, which helped rule out robbery as a motive. And there were no signs of foul play.

The RTP had determined Carradine's death to be accidental and self-inflicted. The cause of death was listed as autoerotic asphyxiation, and the photographs I saw confirmed that theory.

All Carradine did that evening was drink a few vodka sodas at the hotel bar before heading up to his room for the night.

What does the family know?

The piece of evidence on the scene that confirmed the cause of death: David Carradine's personal autoerotic asphyxiation kit. He brought it from home and, according to witnesses, carried it with him on most trips. The kit contained thin, yellow, nylon ropes that were stored in a Crown Royal whiskey bag.

From my investigation, I learned that Carradine had been practicing autoerotic asphyxiation for years. It may have been the reason one of his ex-wives left him. In the divorce papers, she claimed she was troubled by his activities and very dangerous self-harm behavior.

Back to the family. When the Royal Thai Police reported that Carradine had died accidentally by his own hand, the family dismissed it. They claimed foul play.

They must have known about Carradine's taboo (and dangerous) sexual practices, but they didn't want to believe he could have *died* that way. Either that or they simply didn't want it to be true because it would soil his legacy and reputation.

Whatever the reason, the family didn't believe the Royal Thai Police, but everything in my investigation proved they had got it right: David Carradine died of autoerotic asphyxiation.

Setting the record straight

"Good work," my boss said when I delivered the news.

"Thank you," I said, smiling.

"Now I need you to communicate that the Royal Thai Police did their job, and they did it *well*. This case is embarrassing them and making them look bad. Yes, we're here to support the FBI's needs in Thailand, but we are also here to support the local police."

At this point it was Sunday night, and within 24 hours, Director Mueller was scheduled to land in Los Angeles to give an award to Ephraim Zimbalist Jr., the famous star of the old FBI TV show. This is relevant because we knew that while he was in Los Angeles, he would be questioned about the David Carradine case by the local paparazzi. Not only was the *Kill Bill* actor well known there, but the victim's family had specifically asked for the FBI's help.

This detail added urgency to the case. We needed some concrete information to hand Director Mueller to prep him for those questions.

After briefing my supervisor, I planned to head home but found the subway station closed, its entrance barricaded. So I sat on the steps leading down to the station, a quiet spot as good as any, and, using my BlackBerry, typed out the email to Director Mueller.

I didn't interact with Director Mueller directly. I sent the report via email from my BlackBerry, addressing it to him and CCing his staff.

I had met him in passing a couple of times. He had previously served as the US Attorney for the Northern District of California before being nominated as FBI Director by George W. Bush. While I was stationed in the FBI's San Francisco office, I worked with Mueller and his team on a daily basis.

And now I was emailing him about David Carradine.

When I started my email, I mentioned that we had met before, hoping to build a little trust in my report. I know that both he and his staff read it because I received a "thank you" and "job well done" response.

Vindicated

Throughout the entire ordeal, from the moment the Carradine family requested the help of the FBI to their decision to stand down after reading my report that confirmed the initial cause of death, the Royal Thai Police were never vindictive or retaliatory. They didn't bark back at the Carradine family because they didn't want the family to experience further embarrassment. They also wanted to be respectful.

I had so much admiration for the Royal Thai Police *before* the David Carradine case. Their behavior throughout it made me appreciate them even more.

I didn't meet with the Carradine family to deliver the report; that was handled by someone from FBI Headquarters. The most important outcome (from my perspective) was that after the family was briefed, there was no further public criticism of the RTP. The Royal Thai Police were vindicated, and everything went back to normal in Bangkok... until terrorists attacked.

CHAPTER 5

TICK TICK BOOM

IN 2012 AND 2015, THAILAND WAS ATTACKED BY terrorists.

And the FBI was asked to help both times.

I was only involved in specific aspects of each case, from handling translations to being present at the scene. It was my responsibility to provide the FBI with daily updates throughout the investigative process for both cases.

The FBI wasn't always allowed to investigate international terrorist attacks because it didn't have jurisdiction. A case is charged where it happens, so if a crime happens overseas, it is almost always *charged* overseas.

In the 1980s, laws were passed that allowed the FBI to investigate certain crimes overseas. Terrorism is one of them.

It's important to clarify that the US government does not investigate terrorist attacks overseas unless a US citizen is injured or killed or a US entity, such as a US-owned business, military base, or embassy, is damaged. Without these specific connections, the US generally doesn't have jurisdiction to get involved in foreign investigations. However, if a foreign government reaches out and specifically asks for the FBI's help, we almost always say yes.

This is for three reasons.

One, it doesn't matter where it happens; a terrorist attack has the potential to impact an American citizen or an expat living overseas. The US government needs to know about terrorist activity preemptively to protect innocent civilians.

Two, many international terrorist groups target the US. If an attack is orchestrated in Thailand, for example, it is possible that group also has plans to attack the United States. The US government needs to know as much as it can about as many terrorist organizations as possible if it wants to protect as many American citizens, home and abroad, as it can.

And finally, as I had come to realize quickly in Thailand, like with the Carradine case, we want to assist our partners in whatever way we can to help solve cases and bring perpetrators to justice.

The terrorist attacks in Mumbai in 2008, where five Americans died, are a testament to the US government's dedication to international terrorist investigations. The United States has the best databases in the world. Using them, the FBI was able to trace the sale of the engine in the boat used in the bombing to a terrorist organization in Pakistan. It then gave that information to the Indian police to aid in their investigation.

The involvement in these cases helps bring justice for the American deaths and sends a clear message to law enforcement agencies worldwide about the capabilities the US can offer. By allowing us to assist, they see firsthand how fruitful that collaboration can be. It also serves as a warning to terrorists that US law enforcement, particularly the FBI, is everywhere and ready to act, no matter where these events take place. This reinforces our global presence and ensures that those responsible for harming Americans are held accountable.

The two major terror cases I worked while stationed in Thailand were the assassination attempt of an Israeli diplomat in 2012 and the bombing of the Erawan Shrine in 2015.

It was an honor to help investigate them both.

The assassination attempt of the Israeli diplomats

On February 14, 2012, Thailand was the scene of a botched assassination attempt on Israeli diplomats, later referred to as the "Valentine's Day bombs." The day before, similar attempts on similar targets were made in India and Georgia.

But it took a few days to come to that conclusion because when the incident first happened, the reports were confusing. No one reported a terrorist attack; they reported gang violence.

But upon close inspection, that didn't make sense. There was rubble and debris on the scene, and in the middle of the road lay a man on his back; his legs were gone, and it looked like they had been blown off.

The Royal Thai Police found out he was the victim of an accidental bombing. A bomb had gone off inside a nearby house, causing many people to run out. This guy ran out of the house, too, except he was carrying two grenade bombs, one in each hand, when he did.

He lost his legs because of those bombs. When he ran out of the house, he tried to hail a cab. A nearby cab driver turned him down, so he took one of the bombs and rolled it underneath the cab driver's car. Seconds later, it exploded.

The cab driver was injured (the injuries were non-life-threatening), and his cab was badly damaged, which initially drew the attention of the local police, who actively chased the assailant. At one point, the man turned and threw a bomb at them. It hit a tree, bounced off, and ricocheted back toward him before it exploded, blowing off his legs in the process.

Saeed Moradi

This is where I came in.

When the bomb went off inside the house, everyone ran outside, and everyone got away, save one: the guy who blew his legs off.

It didn't take long for the Royal Thai Police to learn this guy's name, Saeed Moradi, and they asked me to find out everything I could about him.

When it comes to cases in the FBI, I learned early in my career that timing is something you can't control. An overseas tour with the FBI always has an end date. And it's always on your mind. Around the time of the Saeed Moradi case, my impending return to the US was approaching faster than I wanted. I was scheduled to leave Thailand the following December because my tour as ALAT Bangkok was ending. Focused on my goal of returning as a legat after a brief stint at FBIHQ, I was actively mapping out a career path that would align with this objective.

I didn't want to leave, even though I had to. I was also stressed trying to figure out where in the US I was going to live when I made it back.

Being asked to step in and help with the investigation was a welcome distraction.

I started by running his name through the database of every US agency, not only the FBI. I didn't find anything. He wasn't in our databases, meaning he wasn't a major *international* terrorist, but I was still motivated to help the Thais figure out the puzzle.

I hit the ground to learn everything I could about Saeed Moradi and anyone else involved in the bombing.

A coordinated attack on Israel

The Royal Thai Police ended up charging five people for the bombing and what we would later learn: the assassination attempt on the Israeli diplomats.

We discovered three of the terrorists flew into Phuket on February 8 and traveled to Pattaya, a beach town, for five nights in the company of three prostitutes. They wanted to party before traveling to Bangkok to meet an older member of the terrorist organization at a private house.He was there to train them on how to make bombs.

But things didn't work out the way they had planned. The older member had been gone only a few hours when one of the bombs they had just made accidentally exploded and blew off part of the roof. We knew this because the Royal Thai Police looked at the CCTV cameras in the vicinity to review footage before the bomb went off.

Almost immediately after the bomb went off in Bangkok, we learned about bombs going off in two other cities the day before: New Delhi, India, and Tbilisi, Georgia. It was then confirmed that the suspects were Iranians, and the nature of the bombs matched a familiar pattern. It became clear that this was part of a larger, organized plan. The bombs were of the same style and followed a similar approach used in other attacks, which helped confirm the connection and the level of coordination involved. An Israeli embassy vehicle was targeted in each instance.

The New Delhi attack occurred just after 3:00 p.m., only a few hundred yards from the Prime Minister's residence, as the Israeli diplomat's wife was on her way to the American Embassy School to pick up her children. As her minivan approached an intersection, she noticed a motorcyclist pull up and attach what appeared to be a magnetic device to her vehicle. Moments later, there was a loud sound, followed by an explosion, and the car caught fire.

The blast left the vehicle charred, blowing out its rear door and causing damage to the car behind it due to the sheer force of the explosion. The woman suffered shrapnel wounds. Her driver, as well as two people in a nearby car, sustained minor injuries.

In Georgia, the situation was similar, but the car bomb was defused in time, and no one was hurt.

Based on that intel, it became clear why the terrorists were in Bangkok: to attack Israeli diplomats living in Thailand. Their plan was to assassinate the diplomats by driving next to embassy vehicles, sticking bombs to the bottom of them, and driving off. Luckily, the terrorists botched their plan.

During the post-blast investigation, we were able to identify key details. From the CCTV footage of the house, we identified five Iranians involved in the plot. One individual was there to teach the others how to make the bombs. Another was responsible for procuring the explosives. Two were there to place the bombs, and the only woman involved had rented the house they were using as their base of operations.

Of the five individuals involved, one was Moradi, the man severely injured when the bomb exploded. Another (Mohammad Hazaei) was caught at the airport in Thailand while attempting to flee the country.

A third suspect (Masoud) was captured in Malaysia as he tried to board a flight to Iran. He went through the extradition process and was ordered to be sent back to Thailand in June of the same year. All three were charged and served time in jail in Thailand.

As for the remaining two, they managed to make it back to Iran, or at least that's what we assume based on the available information. (They wouldn't talk to anyone.)

In November of 2020, Thailand transferred the three Iranians involved in the bomb plot back to Tehran, while Iran released Australian academic Kylie Moore-Gilbert, who had been jailed on espionage charges for over two years. Both sides avoided calling it a prisoner swap, though the Iranians were welcomed as heroes in Tehran.

Bombing the Erawan Shrine

A little over three years later, on August 17, 2015, around rush hour, another bomb went off. It was at the Erawan Shrine, the most symbolic shrine in all of Bangkok, located near the busy Ratchaprasong Intersection in the heart of the city. Surveillance footage captured a suspect leaving a backpack at the scene shortly before the explosion occurred.

The Erawan Shrine sits near the Grand Hyatt Erawan Bangkok, right at the heart of the bustling Ratchaprasong intersection. It's just steps from the BTS Skytrain's Chit Lom Station, which offers a great view of the shrine from its elevated walkway. The area is surrounded by some of Bangkok's biggest shopping malls, including CentralWorld, one of the largest malls in all of Asia.

On most days, the shrine is packed. People come to pray for all kinds of blessings: successful marriages, financial stability, healthy children, good fortune, whatever form that takes.

At the center of it all is a statue of Phra Phrom, the Thai representation of the Hindu god Brahma, seated beneath a tall, ornate canopy. With four faces pointing in different directions, each one symbolizes a virtue: kindness, mercy, sympathy, and impartiality.

All day long and well into the evening, worshippers come and go. Locals and tourists mix in a sort of controlled chaos, part reverent, part curious. Offerings are everywhere: garlands of marigolds, fruit, incense, candles. Traditional Thai dancers often perform on-site, typically hired by those hoping that a dance offered in gratitude will help their prayers come true.

Even as the shrine radiates a peaceful energy, the city around it never slows down. Just beyond its gates, traffic roars by, Skytrains hum overhead, and shoppers flow in and out of glittering malls. It's a perfect Bangkok contradiction: spirituality and modern life coexisting in constant motion.

While there is a history of bombings in the restive southern region of Thailand, this particular bombing in Bangkok was the largest the city had ever seen, resulting in the most casualties and injuries. Witnessing the aftermath firsthand was both sobering and surreal.

The explosion was huge. The bomb had been placed under a metal bench, which increased the impact of the blast; the bench was left blackened and was disproportionately twisted in one direction. This placement, and the layout of the shrine, helped direct the force of the explosion outward toward the shrine and the Hyatt Erawan Hotel, which took the brunt of the blast. Most of the hotel's windows were shattered, and the hotel facade received significant damage. Just behind the bench is a BTS Skytrain track and a pedestrian walkway, both of which were also impacted. The glass panels along the walkway were shattered in several spots, and the structure itself was impacted.

Multiple casualties

I got the report of the incident right away: there were multiple injured and multiple casualties on the scene. I was nearby, a quick 10-minute sprint up the street, so when I arrived, the scene was still mayhem, and I was struck by it. There were bodies and debris everywhere.

Amid the chaos, the Manager of the Hyatt Erawan reached out to me and the Regional Security Officer after failing to connect with the Thai police. Some body parts had made it so far they were strewn across the Hyatt's rooftop pool deck.

"Help me; I have body parts in my pool."

Realizing the gravity of the situation, I immediately called the Thai authorities, urging them to respond to his calls.

I quickly reached out to my local contacts as well as FBI headquarters and told them what I saw. We later found out there were 14 fatalities, and none were from the US; they were all from Thailand, Malaysia, Indonesia, and other ethnically Chinese countries.

All the while, along with the other law enforcement personnel on the scene, I kept a safe distance, just in case a second bomb went off. We had no way of knowing whether one of the deceased was the bomber or if he was luring us in to strike (even bigger) again.

The RTP reviewed the CCTV tapes but did not arrest anyone. So a weeklong manhunt began…something the FBI was ready and able to help with.

Catching a terrorist

Royal Thai Police investigators said they were "certain" that a man caught on a security camera leaving a backpack at the explosion site was responsible for the blast. The footage, which was broadcast internationally, showed the man wearing shorts and a yellow T-shirt. He sat on a bench, took off a dark-colored backpack, placed it underneath the bench, and walked away.

Thailand's chief of police stated that the attack was the work of a larger criminal network and released a sketch of the "unidentified foreign man" seen in the CCTV footage. A warrant for his arrest was issued on the same day a reward was announced.

The Royal Thai Police wanted the FBI's help because they wanted to know which terrorist organization orchestrated the attack. They were concerned Thailand's southern insurgency was attempting to expand into the north. They were afraid a Thai person from the south was bombing Bangkok.

The southern insurgency was largely seen as a domestic conflict. No outside countries had wanted to, or felt the need to, get involved, which is typical in these kinds of situations around the world. The three southern provinces are predominantly Muslim, unlike the rest of the country, which is mainly Buddhist, so not many foreigners live there. However, the Thai government understood that if the conflict spread to Bangkok, they wouldn't be able to prevent international attention and involvement.

There was a lot of speculation, with daily reports about who "might" have been involved, and plenty of talking heads in the media. It was the top story on CNN and made headlines around the world. Thailand, being one of the top tourist destinations globally for many years, was especially concerned about the impact this could have on its tourism industry.

The driver of a tuk-tuk (a three-wheeled motorized vehicle used as a taxi and ubiquitous in Thailand) later came forward, confirming he had picked up the suspect. He described the man as "not in a hurry. He seemed to be calm, like a regular customer, and not Thai. He also spoke in an unclear language."

On August 29, 2015, police arrested a 28-year-old man in connection with the bombing. While he was not believed to be the bomber, he was suspected of being involved. His nationality was unclear, but he possessed a fake Turkish passport, along with at least 11 other Turkish passports and over 200 passports in total at his apartment, along with bomb-making materials.

The following day, August 30, authorities raided another apartment building in Bangkok, uncovering more bomb-making components. They issued arrest warrants for 26-year-old Wanna Suansan, who was living in Turkey, and a foreign man named Jusuf.

It took two weeks of diligent investigation to piece it all together: the attack on the Erawan Shrine was likely linked to a Turkish group. Thai authorities claimed that the bombings were carried out by a Turkish ultranationalist group in retaliation for Thailand's decision to deport Uyghur terrorist suspects back to China rather than allowing them to seek asylum in Turkey. A Chinese ethnic Uyghur man, Adem Karadag, 31, was arrested by Thai police in connection with the bombing after they found fake Turkish passports and bomb-making materials in his apartment.

The attack was massive news, and the pressure was intense right from the start, especially as we waited to learn the nationalities of the victims. When we found out there were no US citizens among them, the pressure eased a bit. But for me, this was the biggest event of my career.

What made this case feel different was the sense of responsibility I felt toward the Thai people, especially my Thai and expat friends. They had always been interested in my work, but now I could see they were feeling vulnerable and scared, looking to me for some reassurance.

I had worked 9/11, so I had experience with being attacked. My Thai friends and colleagues had never been through anything like this. They were worried about getting attacked again.

I felt a bit like, *John, this is what you do, so get it done and make them feel safe.*

It was my job to reassure them that when an attack like this happens, the authorities are on their toes. That's what happened after 9/11, and it was what was going to happen in Bangkok too.

And recent events validated those suspicions. Thailand had recently deported Chinese Uyghur leaders back to China, a move that was condemned by many human rights groups that believed they should have been deported to Turkey, where they would get help. It is widely believed that the Chinese government is committing ongoing human rights abuses against Uyghurs and other ethnic and religious minorities in Xinjiang, often described as persecution or even genocide. In China, Uyghurs faced the threat of persecution and imprisonment. This belief is shared by many, including the US government.

It appeared as though the bombing was retaliation for the deportation.

Adem Karadag

I partnered with the RTP throughout their investigation. While there was no direct US connection (no suspects with US ties, no US victims, and nothing connecting the motive to US interests), my Thai police colleagues wanted the FBI involved. I was more than eager to oblige. We made discoveries and chased leads together.

Based on our suspicions, we zeroed in on Adem Karadag, an Uyghur with ties to the Chinese community. The RTP arrested him at his apartment in Bangkok and found a stockpile of fake Turkish passports and bomb-making materials. Each search they conducted led to new avenues to explore. The Thai authorities did a great job of using one piece of evidence to uncover the next, methodically building the case that eventually led them to Adem.

While searching, they also found notebooks with a significant amount of evidence written in the Uyghur language, a tongue unfamiliar to the RTP.

This is where I came in.

Uyghur is a very rare language spoken by very few, so it was a stroke of luck that I located a DEA employee in New York City who spoke it. I expedited the transfer of notebooks containing crucial information for review.

The information contained in the notebooks advanced the Thai's investigation. They not only confirmed the initial suspicions regarding the involvement of Uyghur individuals but also shed light on the motives behind the bombings.

The Uyghurs

Of all terrorist attacks around the world, 99.9% are typically linked to a group that the US is concerned about, or at least the US is tracking some area of the group's movements and/or members. In 2015, the Uyghurs weren't on the FBI's radar, and initially we couldn't find Adem anywhere, and there seemed to be little connection to the US, which made it hard to assist my Thai counterparts in understanding the motivation behind the attack on the shrine.

Karadag did admit his involvement at first but later retracted his confession. Because of this, the Thais couldn't get to the bigger players behind the case. As of now, he and a co-conspirator are the only ones charged for the actual bombing (in 2024, the court cleared a woman accused of involvement).

Our ability to help the investigation hit a roadblock because the group wasn't a known threat to Americans.

In the end, though, the FBI was instrumental in ensuring that the perpetrators were brought to justice. The Thai authorities had caught the right guy.

At the time of writing this book, Karadag and his co-conspirator were awaiting trial.

Restoring the shrine

By August 19, the debris from the Erawan Shrine had been completely cleared, and it was back to business as usual. There was an urgent need to restore the tourist location quickly, and I was as impressed by the swift response as I was to the thoroughness of the investigation.

Investigating these cases isn't easy. The Boston Marathon bombing investigation famously had more mobile phone videos and pictures than any event in history, which was a huge help to us. In contrast, this bombing had limited CCTV coverage, making the manhunt much more challenging. The fact that they managed to catch the bomber within a few weeks was truly impressive.

My first experience with terrorism as an FBI agent was 9/11. I'd only been an agent for two years at that point. Over the years, I hadn't directly handled a terrorist attack myself, but I played a small role in the Boston Marathon case and worked on other cases in a more peripheral way. Even though these attacks in Bangkok didn't directly impact the US, they hit me hard because they happened in a city I covered, lived in, and felt connected to. My Thai friends didn't feel the pain of 9/11 in the same way. For them, Erawan was their 9/11.

I knew, after both incidents, that no matter how I felt, people looked to the US as the "experts" in handling these kinds of crises. We'd dealt with major attacks before, and we did it with professionalism, speed, and a skill set that was respected around the world. When the Erawan bombing suspects were caught, I felt a sense of relief knowing I had played a part in it, and I was proud of my Thai colleagues for their hard work.

CHAPTER 6

THE MARINE

AS AN FBI AGENT WORKING INTERNATIONALLY, I OFTEN dealt with extradition, a formal process where one country requests the return of a person to face trial or serve a sentence for a crime. Though the concept seems straightforward, in reality, it involves navigating a complex interplay of legal, diplomatic, and international protocols.

Extradition challenges are deeply tied to geopolitical relations and the specific laws of the countries involved. A key principle here is "dual criminality," which requires the act in question be recognized as a crime in both countries. This often complicates or stalls the process when what is considered a severe offense in one country might not be recognized as such in another.

In my time in Thailand, dual criminality has come up frequently. When I first receive an investigative assistance request from an agent, it is the first thing I think about. If there's no dual criminality between the US and Thailand, I can do some preliminary work, but I make sure to inform the requesting agent early on that assistance will be limited. A prime example I encountered often, especially in my early days, was parental kidnapping cases. The US has a specific federal law against international parental kidnapping, but Thailand doesn't have any such law, there's not even a law against parental kidnapping domestically. So with no dual criminality, we were stuck.

But then we started thinking outside the box. By working closely with the Thai police, the Embassy Consular section, and other entities, we found a way forward. When someone has an outstanding arrest warrant, their passport becomes eligible for revocation. Once it was revoked, we could inform the Thai police, who would then invalidate the person's visa, making them eligible for deportation. The FBI would go through this process, and the Royal Thai Police would arrest the fugitive and begin the deportation process. In the end, I would often fly back to the US with the fugitive, where they would be arrested upon landing.

The entire process involves more than just legal documentation; it requires coordination across multiple government agencies and an intricate, diplomatic dance between entities like the State Department and foreign ministries. Managing these steps is a difficult task, filled with delays and political complexities that can prolong the extradition process.

Understanding these nuances is crucial, as they influence not only the outcome of individual cases but also broader international relations and the enforcement of global justice. Extradition does not merely begin with a legal request; it plays out on a complex stage of international law and bilateral negotiations, complicating what might initially appear as a straightforward procedure.

A landmark case

I was involved in the first-ever agreement by England to extradite a citizen to Thailand. This landmark case set a significant precedent in international law. This incident highlighted significant gaps in international law enforcement and underscored the importance of international cooperation.

The case centered on Lee Aldhouse, a British national who, after an altercation in a Phuket bar, fatally stabbed Dashawn Longfellow, a former US Marine.

Phuket is full of all types of bars and discos, but the kind of bar we're talking about here would be similar to what an

American might imagine as a cross between a dive bar and a beach bar. It's a standard setup, lots of wooden tables, rattan chairs, a couple of pool tables, and a stage for live bands, all open to the tropical Phuket air. It's the kind of place where you'd find plenty of male tourists and Thai women hanging out.

Longfellow's girlfriend testified that she was a waitress at the Freedom Bar on Rawai Beach. On August 14, 2010, at around 1:20 a.m., Longfellow arrived at the bar to pick her up and take her back to their apartment.

There were only about 10 people left in the bar by the time Longfellow arrived, as it was nearing closing time. While waiting, he sat at a table with another tourist but didn't order anything. At 1:40 a.m., Aldhouse pulled up on a dark-green motorbike, came into the bar looking visibly angry, ordered a beer, and sat at a different table.

By 2:00 a.m., Aldhouse began talking loudly, as if he was angry with the remaining customers, because he challenged every one of them to a fight. During this, Longfellow got up to go to the restroom, but Aldhouse blocked his way and then punched Longfellow in the face. Other customers tried to intervene, but Aldhouse attacked them as well before leaving the bar.

Longfellow's girlfriend further testified that one of her friends saw Aldhouse walk into a 7-Eleven, 100 meters away, and buy a knife. Her friend then advised her to take Longfellow home immediately, but after returning to their apartment, Longfellow went to a nearby shop for water.

Around 3:30 a.m., Longfellow came home, but as he did, he knocked one of the apartment's sliding glass doors off its rocker. As they were fixing it, Aldhouse showed up again, now wearing a black hoodie. He approached Longfellow and stabbed him twice in the chest. Despite Longfellow telling his girlfriend to go inside, she tried to defend him by throwing a clothes rack at Aldhouse. Aldhouse taunted her before fleeing when she called for help.

Rescue workers arrived around 5:00 a.m., but unfortunately, they were unable to revive Longfellow.

Aldhouse then fled the country to avoid apprehension. To make his escape, he exploited less stringent border controls and crossed into Cambodia. His route through Cambodia was strategic, utilizing the gaps in international law enforcement and border security that often exist between less closely monitored border points. This allowed him to evade Thai authorities temporarily and make his way back to England.

Aldhouse was apprehended at Heathrow Airport upon his arrival in the UK due to an existing warrant for his arrest. This warrant was issued after he left the country while on bail for a prior offense. This arrest for a different crime was the key to giving authorities in Thailand time to get their paperwork in order.

The process and the challenge

From the moment the crime was reported, the extradition process was prioritized. The suspect fled Thailand via Cambodia before returning to England, adding layers of complexity to the efforts to bring Aldhouse to face justice in Thailand. Each step had to be meticulously documented and justified. It required not only understanding the legal framework but also engaging in sensitive negotiations that could affect international relations.

US involvement in the Aldhouse case began not after

his arrest but when the Attorney General's Office received documentation from the British government indicating that Aldhouse was contesting his extradition.

They reached out to me personally. "A US Marine died. The FBI needs to help us."

Although this type of case was not typically within our purview, my decision to assist was influenced by my professional relationship with Prosecutor Intranee Sumawong, Executive Director of International Affairs in the Office of the Attorney General for Thailand (Thai AG's Office). We had collaborated on many cases before, and her request for help was all I needed to commit. In this particular case, Thailand didn't need to prove Aldhouse's guilt during the extradition process. A common misconception is that the requesting country has to prove guilt, but really, they only need to establish probable cause that the individual in question is the one who committed the crime. It's about proving identity and showing that the crime meets the dual criminality standard. The British and Thai authorities handled all of that.

One significant precondition from the British government impacted the Aldhouse case even before the extradition battle commenced. The UK has a standing rule against extraditing a citizen to a country where they may face the death penalty. Consequently, before the extradition proceedings could progress, the Thai authorities were required to assure that Aldhouse would face no more than life imprisonment if extradited, and they did.

Once those steps are completed, the individual has the right to challenge the extradition for a number of reasons. One common argument is that the individual might face cruel and unusual punishment if convicted. That was exactly where Aldhouse focused his fight. According to my sources, he was familiar with a documentary about the poor conditions in Thai prisons, and he and his legal team used examples from that show to argue against his extradition.

They provided detailed documentation and precedents in extradition law to bolster their case, ensuring every legal avenue was explored to counter the defense's narrative.

Persuading the Brits

A crucial moment in the extradition process involved persuading British authorities of the validity and urgency of the extradition request. This effort required the AG's office to present a compelling legal case while diplomatically addressing concerns about Aldhouse's potential treatment in Thailand. The negotiations needed to reassure the UK of Thailand's commitment to international human rights standards without compromising national sovereignty.

When the RTP tracked Aldhouse's movements, they shared information with both Cambodia and England. They also had informal dialogues and built rapport with counterparts in various countries, interactions that were critical for easing potential diplomatic tensions and promoting a collaborative approach throughout the investigative process.

To clarify, I wasn't involved in locating Aldhouse. The fact that the victim was an American doesn't automatically bring US authorities into the case. If a Brit killed a Thai citizen in New York City, the British and American authorities would handle the case and the extradition process. The Thais could show interest, but their involvement would likely be minimal or nonexistent.

Secondly, I want to make clear what my role actually was.

I didn't conduct on-site inspections, nor did I collect evidence or organize visits for outside observers. I helped the AG's office prove their prison system was up to British standards. And this assistance turned out to be more important than I could have imagined.

I did that by first meeting with Sumawong.

Thai prison conditions

I was up to speed on the Aldhouse case as much as most people were, from news reports and a little from my British and Thai police colleagues. However, while I was definitely paying closer attention due to Longfellow being an American citizen and his Marine Corps background, I had no belief the FBI would get involved. The case was progressing into an area where US authorities would monitor the case of a US citizen as the victim but not assist in the case in a hands-on manner.

That all changed when Intranee contacted me.

The phone rang in my office, and Intranee yelled her normal greeting: "Khun John, my best friend!" She then told me that she needed help on the Aldhouse case and asked if I could drop everything and go see her in her office. Intranee and I had a great working relationship, so I jumped in my car and headed to the AG's office.

When I arrived, Intranee and one of her line attorneys were in the room. The line attorney had his laptop out. She asked me to sit down and told me they were in a tough spot.

Naturally, I asked why.

She explained that they had just received a document from the UK court outlining Aldhouse's defense team's petition to block extradition. The defense was arguing that if Aldhouse were extradited and found guilty of Longfellow's murder, he would be subject to cruel and unusual punishment in Thailand's prisons.

I asked what she wanted me to do, reminding her that this wasn't an FBI case. But she knew exactly how to get me involved.

"Don't you want to help get justice for a former Marine?" Well, that was an immediate yes. The legat job is never black and white. Helping on this investigation was actually a choice. There are definitely legats who would have chosen to remind Thai authorities that the FBI has no jurisdiction in this case and that it is a matter between the Thai and UK governments.

Not me. I asked how I could assist, and she had her assistant read the petition aloud.

Article 3 of the European Convention on Human Rights

Aldhouse's defense team centered their arguments around Article 3 of the European Convention on Human Rights, which prohibits torture and inhumane treatment. They claimed that the size and conditions in Thai prisons violated these standards.

While I'd been in many Thai (and US) jails, I had never given much thought to cell sizes or whether they met international standards (and, frankly, I wouldn't even know what those standards were).

So I asked Intranee, "Do they?"

She admitted she had no idea.

I then told her we needed someone to measure the jail cell. Since the murder took place on the Thai island of Phuket, and that was where Aldhouse would be housed if found guilty, I asked her to reach out to the prison there.

With one phone call, we had the warden of the Phuket prison on the line. Intranee explained the situation to him.

I asked, "What size are the cells?"

Intranee relayed the question in Thai. The warden was then adamant that the cells met international minimum standards, but I could hear the uncertainty in his voice.

Trying to keep my tone as neutral as possible, I said, "He needs to get a tape measure, walk into the cell, and measure it."

And that was exactly what happened. As we listened, the warden of the largest prison in Phuket grabbed a tape measure, walked into the cell, and measured it.

Turned out the cell was up to international standards.

I could tell that Intranee, her assistant, and the warden were all a little dumbfounded by the current turn of events. I have to say, I was truly making it up as I went along. Had I ever responded to a petition fighting extradition? No. So I really just did what I thought was logical: take each argument one by one and answer them all with cold, hard facts.

Aldhouse's second claim was that Thai prisoners are served fish heads for every meal.

So I asked, "Are they?"

The warden laughed. "No. Of course not!"

I followed up. "Well, what are they served?" Again, I didn't get a specific answer. So I pressed on. "Warden, do you have a cook in charge of the prison food?"

The warden answered, "Of course."

"Does he make a menu?"

"Yes."

"Can he send us this week's menu?"

"Right away," the warden said.

And finally, just to be sure, I asked, "Are there fish heads on this week's menu?"

Luckily, the answer was no, there weren't.

After we cleared up that second claim, my colleagues were fully on board. We were able to systematically dismantle each and every one of Aldhouse's bogus accusations.

This legal strategy highlighted the role of human rights in extradition challenges, making the proceedings particularly contentious. The focus on these conditions reflected broader cultural assumptions and biases, adding another layer of complexity to the already difficult diplomatic and legal negotiations.

It was one of those "they don't teach this in the academy" moments that I had during my time in Thailand.

One of the most rewarding moments of my entire FBI career came when my phone rang, and it was Intranee. She told me that the petition had failed, and Aldhouse was already on a plane back to Thailand. My work was instrumental in that result.

The Aldhouse extradition demonstrated the critical role of diplomacy in law enforcement; it emphasized the need for tact, cultural sensitivity, and strategic negotiation skills. These efforts were not just about adhering strictly to the extradition treaty but about creating a cooperative environment that could manage the complexities of a high-profile international legal case.

The court of public opinion

The Aldhouse case was public and scrutinized, which placed significant pressure on all parties to maintain transparency and fairness. Each of our arguments needed to be meticulously presented and substantiated.

But the battle over Aldhouse's extradition was being tried

in the court of public opinion, too, where the integrity of Thai justice was being called into question.

In Thailand, whenever the Royal Thai Police or the criminal justice system are in the spotlight, there's always a segment of society that doesn't trust the system. Even today, post-retirement, I spend a lot of time explaining that the RTP is filled with dedicated, capable officers. Similarly, when I'd talk about my involvement in this case, people would often tell me they believed Thailand was nowhere near compliant with international standards.

In the court of public opinion, the dynamic is complicated. While you'd expect the public to focus on sympathy for Longfellow's family and outrage toward the man who allegedly murdered him in cold blood, there was an underlying tone of sympathy for Aldhouse because he'd be facing life in a Thai prison. To prove to the public that the Thai justice system worked, extradition proceedings needed to be well planned for and transparent, so we remained committed to upholding both the precise requirements and broader principles of international law. We worked hard to balance the pursuit of justice with respect for national sovereignty.

I don't think the pressure came from mistrust during the process as much as from the urgency to get this right. We had a murdered American Marine, and while I'm not saying Aldhouse's guilt was guaranteed, we had more than enough evidence to justify his extradition so he could stand trial. It was a straightforward case in that sense, and we couldn't afford to mess it up.

If my Thai colleagues and I couldn't at least prove that much, it would have been seen as a failure, and that could have fueled the public's distrust in the Thai police. Over the years, there have been instances where the Thai government has been perceived as not being able to "finish the job" in certain cases, and we definitely didn't want this to become another of those examples.

Community impact

The Aldhouse extradition deeply impacted communities in both Thailand and the United States; it resonated emotionally with local communities and stirred significant international law enforcement interest. In Phuket, where the crime occurred, the incident brought to light the unsettling reality of international crime, challenging the local police and community to prevent their vibrant tourist hub from becoming a refuge for international fugitives.

In the United States, the repercussions hit the veteran and active military communities hard. Dashawn Longfellow's service in Iraq and Afghanistan (marked by his receipt of a Purple Heart) made his death a deeply personal issue for those with similar backgrounds. Veteran groups and military organizations intensely pursued justice, seeking closure for a fallen comrade whose tragedy transcended national boundaries.

The Aldhouse extradition strengthened community bonds and fostered a collaborative spirit in law enforcement efforts.

The emotional response from these communities emphasized the broader societal effects of the case. It extended beyond legalities to address the collective mourning of a respected hero, magnified by extensive media coverage that highlighted the complexities of managing international crimes. This public attention influenced safety and security discussions, especially in tourist areas frequented by international visitors, prompting a reevaluation of security measures and enhanced international law enforcement cooperation.

It also initiated important discussions on justice, public safety, and the need for strong legal and diplomatic strategies to manage cross-border crime. The involvement of local communities added depth to the narrative; it painted a comprehensive picture of the extradition process and its wide-reaching consequences on global communities.

Strong sense of duty

The desire to serve Dashawn Longfellow's family in the pursuit of justice was a significant driving force for everyone involved in the case, especially the law enforcement teams: the Royal Thai Police and the legat Bangkok office. Our motivation went beyond the standard professional obligation; it was deeply personal and ethical because Longfellow had served his country as a US Marine. His untimely death in a foreign country due to a violent crime invoked a strong sense of duty among all of us.

Triumph of justice

Ultimately, our perseverance paid off. Lee Aldhouse lost his appeal and was extradited back to Thailand. This marked a significant victory because the extradition followed intense diplomatic efforts and legal battles across continents. It set a precedent for handling major international crimes.

Aldhouse was sentenced to 25 years in prison when he returned to Thailand. This sentence continues to serve as a deterrent to others who might consider evading justice by crossing borders. International borders do not protect criminals from justice. Perpetrators are held accountable, and victims' families see justice served.

The successful extradition and sentencing of Aldhouse demonstrated the effectiveness of international collaboration to overcome legal and logistical challenges, and the impact of this case extended beyond the courtroom; it strengthened ties between the nations involved, showcased the importance of perseverance and commitment to justice across borders, and emphasized our ability to collaborate on future legal matters.

It also emphasized the need for a grieving family to see justice for their loss. The extradition was more than a procedural success; it was an act of restitution for a family shattered by violence, driven by the need to provide closure to fallen Marine Dashawn Longfellow's loved ones.

The Aldhouse extradition case is an example of why I fight for justice, regardless of the challenges.

CHAPTER 7

NOWHERE TO RUN

A FUGITIVE IS SOMEONE WHO IS WANTED BY THE LAW, meaning there is a warrant out for their arrest. When someone leaves the jurisdiction from which the arrest warrant is issued, they are considered a fugitive.

In fiscal year 2023, the US Marshals Service arrested 73,362 fugitives. This includes 28,065 arrests on federal warrants and 45,297 on state and local warrants. On average, the Marshals made 293 arrests per operational day.[3] The number of fugitives apprehended often involves individuals wanted for serious crimes such as sex offenses, gang activities, and homicides. For example, they arrested over 10,000 sex offenders and more than 5,400 homicide suspects during this period.[4]

In 2023, the US Marshals also handled 1,487 international or foreign fugitive cases. These cases involve individuals wanted by other nations but believed to be in the United States.[5] Additionally, the US Marshals facilitated 772 international removals, including extraditions, deportations, and expulsions, highlighting the collaborative effort between the US and other countries in handling fugitives.[6]

Many local law enforcement agencies, a.k.a. your local county and state police, only have enough budget to bring someone back across adjacent state lines, meaning they rarely have the money to find and bring home an international fugitive. While some are local or state fugitives, many are also FBI fugitives.

---

[3] U.S. Marshals Service, "2024 Facts and Figures" (Washington, DC: U.S. Department of Justice, 2024), https://www.usmarshals.gov/sites/default/files/media/document/2024-Facts-and-Figures.pdf.

[4] U.S. Marshals Service, "2024 Facts and Figures."

[5] U.S. Marshals Service, "2024 Facts and Figures."

[6] "US Marshals Service: Fugitive Investigations, US Marshals Service, accessed June 26, 2025, https://www.usmarshals.gov/what-we-do/fugitive-investigations.

Regardless, the agency is usually called to help with international fugitive cases because it has funds to help bring the wanted person home. The US Marshals office has the funds, too, but because the FBI has offices all over the world, it has more resources to assist with international fugitive cases.

Why do fugitives go to Thailand?

When you arrive in Thailand, visitors from many countries, including the US, automatically receive a 30-day stay, sometimes even longer. After those 30 days, you're supposed to leave, but it's easy to get another 30 days. And after 60 days, many people do what's called a "visa run," leaving the country for a neighboring one and then reentering to get a fresh 30-day stamp. You can do this several times. As long as you keep a low profile and don't do anything to attract attention from the police or immigration, no one is actively checking on you…unless they are, which is where foreign police looking for fugitives come into play.

It's worth noting that Customs and Immigration are separate agencies in Thailand. When you enter, you're asked to inform Immigration about where you'll be staying, but they rarely verify that.

As for the cost of living, Thailand is ranked among the best countries for expats, with the cost of living being about 2.6 times lower than in the US. You can expect to spend anywhere from $650 to $3,000 per month, depending on your lifestyle. Some can live on much less, and some spend much more. Any lifestyle you want to live, Thailand can accommodate.

The FBI and international fugitives

When the FBI is enlisted in international fugitive cases, one of the first questions we ask is whether the agency asking for help has enough money to bring their fugitive home. The second thing we ask is for access to all the information they have on the fugitive so we have an idea of where to start to look. Many times, they know very little about the fugitive in question.

"He's a white guy living somewhere in Pattaya. He's teaching English."

It's a common misconception among agents unfamiliar with Thailand that finding a Westerner here will be easy. They assume there are only a few *hundred* Westerners here and that a foreigner will stand out. And when a fugitive is hiding outside Bangkok, they think a smaller city means an even easier search. But the reality is far from that simple: there are *tens* of thousands of Westerners here.

In truth, smaller cities like Pattaya or Chiang Mai are filled with Westerners blending into the vibrant expat communities.

So one of the first things I did as the FBI's ALAT was to educate the agencies that enlisted me, or the FBI case agent, on how much information they needed to get started.

I often suggest agents take a look at these cities on YouTube, where they'll see a constant stream of Western faces. It's a stark reminder that the same level of detail—an address, a phone number—is just as essential in Thailand as it would be in Chicago or Detroit. A name alone is never enough.

There is, however, one advantage here that we don't have back in the States: the power of a passport number. With the right connections in Immigration, a single passport number can reveal whether someone has entered the country and whether they've left. And many times, that passport helps with other investigative steps related to where a fugitive may be hiding. It's a small piece of information, but it can make all the difference, giving us a clear signal that the search is worth pursuing.

But maintaining operational secrecy is vital, especially in locations like Phuket and Pattaya, where long-term residents have likely established local connections. These fugitives may warn their acquaintances to alert them about any inquiries, possibly under the guise of avoiding stalkers or protecting their children from perceived threats. Therefore, we operate with a level of discretion that ensures our approach remains unsuspected. This isn't merely about apprehension; it's about managing the entire scenario discreetly to facilitate a smooth and effective resolution.

Are you familiar with the movie *The Departed*, starring Leonardo DiCaprio, Jack Nicholson, and Matt Damon? It's loosely based on a gangster named Whitey Bulger, who was in hiding for 20 years. It was assumed he had fled the country. One of the countries intelligence listed was Thailand... and throughout the years, we had many, many "sightings." As legat Bangkok, I was required to follow up on every one. (There were at least a dozen. There are a lot of 60-year-old white men in Thailand.)

Turns out, though, he had never left LA. He was arrested in his apartment, where he had been hiding the entire time.

Fugitive case #1: The Irish mobster

My entry into the field of international fugitive recovery began with a case concerning an alleged Irish gangster. To prepare, I met with a renowned colleague, General Preecha Thimontri, a.k.a. General Oud.

I was introduced to General Oud by a former boss; he had graduated from the FBI National Academy and had become not only a respected colleague but also a close friend. When I briefed him about the case (which involved a figure reminiscent of Whitey Bulger but with notable differences), his interest was immediately engaged. The suspect, a man in his 60s living in Thailand, was wanted for racketeering, money laundering, and assault.

In 2009, about a year into my role, I began the detailed work of tracking the mobster. With General Oud's help, we went through his immigration papers to follow his movements since arriving in Thailand. An agent found that the mobster had contacted someone in the United States, providing us with phone data that was outdated yet vital. I suggested to General Oud that we could use this data, possibly with the phone company's assistance, to find him.

The next day, General Oud and I, along with his fugitive team, reassessed the case. It was remarkable how quickly General Oud managed to obtain the phone data, pointing us toward the likely area where the fugitive was hiding. (The Thai police, experienced in handling such cases, were able to access these records much faster than normal.) My task was to provide as much supportive information as possible to aid his efforts.

The pace of the case quickened unexpectedly. Within hours after implementing our strategy, General Oud called to inform me that the fugitive had been apprehended. He had been moving from one hotel to another with his Thai girlfriend, trying to evade capture. But sharp instincts and timely intelligence led General Oud and his team directly to them before they could get away again.

Extradition, the return journey, and my preflight ritual

After the arrest, I took on the role of interviewing the alleged gangster, discussing his options with him. Confronted with the choice between a prolonged extradition battle in a Thai prison and immediate deportation to the US, he chose the latter. So we began the deportation process.

The process we use when bypassing formal extradition and opting for deportation is a bit unique. It starts with the US State Department making the fugitive's passport "revocable" rather than fully revoked. This might seem like a minor detail, but it's crucial. In some countries, being caught without a valid passport can lead to immediate detention or worse, and the US aims to avoid putting its citizens in that kind of jeopardy. By keeping the passport technically revocable, the Thai government can move forward with revoking the fugitive's visa.

Once that happens, the fugitive is given a choice: remain in Thai immigration detention until they can personally cover the cost of a one-way ticket to the United States (the only country Thai authorities will permit them to travel to), or accept a US government-funded ticket and be deported with official assistance.

The FBI covers the cost of my round-trip ticket back to the US, and I take my place next to the fugitive on the flight. Technically, they aren't in my custody, but I keep that under wraps. I inform them that upon landing, they'll be taken into custody by US authorities.

For the duration of the flight, the Thai Airways crew assumes I'm responsible for them. The fugitive assumes they're in my custody. And really, for all intents and purposes, they are. The reality is, though, that until the fugitive sets foot on US soil, they technically can't be taken into custody.

But once we're on that plane, they've got nowhere to go.

An eye-opening conversation with the Assistant US Attorney at the embassy during my time in Thailand made it clear: legally speaking, it's a total gray area.

While some cases allow for the US Marshals Service to assist with transporting fugitives, for the most part, the FBI is tasked with handling the logistics and physical escorting of the fugitive.

This was my first solo prisoner deportation. I was given some useful hints and advice from a few current and former legats in the Asia region as to how to handle the long-haul process; however, I knew I needed to set up a routine for a process that I would have to repeat many times during my overseas assignment.

I knew I needed to be cordial enough with the fugitive so they would not have any desire to make the flight an uncomfortable experience for both of us. Before takeoff, regardless of who they are, I treat them to a meal. I give them a choice of a few places...and they always pick Burger King. I guess some things are common among all Americans, including the love of fast food.

It's likely their last taste of freedom for a while, and I pay for it out of pocket. This small act of kindness is part of maintaining civility, no matter the individual's past.

At the airport, I handle security personally.

When conducting a search before boarding a plane, the scrutiny is far more intense than a standard police search for weapons or dangerous items. The stricter regulations on what can be carried onto a flight demand a heightened level of attention. This is why I take an extra step, conducting a more thorough search: it's not just about finding something suspicious; it's about ensuring nothing dangerous slips through in an environment where the stakes are higher.

This includes a meticulous check of their shoes and clothing. After this, I explain what to expect during the flight and upon landing. This includes the explanation that while the fugitive is not going to be handcuffed (airline rules don't allow for handcuffing), I have them at the ready, in case I need to use them. The fugitive is told I will have the airline staff take away any sharp objects (like a knife with the meal) but that they will be free to sleep, eat, watch a movie, etc. As long as they are good to me, I will be good to them. My job at this point is to get the fugitive from point A to point B. And I have built a routine that has made arriving safely and without incident a priority.

It is important to explain that for all my fugitive returns to the US, we took commercial airline flights. While I was in Bangkok, Thai Airways always had a direct flight from Bangkok to LAX. In recent years, that flight makes a stop in Korea, adding a layer of complexity due to the need to coordinate with another government to transfer the fugitive from one plane to another.

Once aboard, I adopt a strict no-sleep policy for myself to ensure constant vigilance, while allowing the detainees to rest. Interaction varies. Some detainees are more talkative, and in such cases, I might resort to headphones to maintain my focus and sanity during the long flights. A smooth and trouble-free flight back to the US is critical.

When we touch down, typically at LAX, agents from the US CBP and FBI and sometimes an officer from the LA County Sheriff's Office or LAPD may be part of the arrest team. It's a seamless process, blending diplomacy and law enforcement to ensure everything goes by the book.

For the Irish gangster, I explained that cooperating would be in his best interest, even hinting that if he behaved, he might get bail. (That was a bold-faced lie; he was never going to make bail.) The flight proceeded without incident, and upon arrival, the critical part of my role was to ensure that the law enforcement officers boarding the plane did not confuse me with the fugitive, as I wasn't wearing anything that would identify me as a law enforcement officer. It isn't an exact science, and coordination via mobile phone as we land is a key component of making sure there are no mistakes. I was able to manage the situation without any problems.

Once landed, the Irish gangster was escorted away in handcuffs.

On a side note, this handoff was memorable because the Irish gangster was dressed to the nines when I handed him to the local team. He had changed into a suit in the bathroom before we landed because he expected fanfare and press. Neither ever arrived.

Was he disappointed? I don't know. He never showed a hint of emotion, like a true gangster.

Fugitive case #2: the parental kidnapper

Parental kidnapping is a unique challenge, especially in international cases. As I noted in the extradition chapter, there must be dual criminality for the FBI to get involved; the act must be considered a crime in both Thailand and the US. In such instances, extradition isn't possible, only deportation.

This case began with a call from a South Carolina–based FBI agent. A father who had only limited visitation rights had deceived the mother by claiming to take their child to Disney World. By Monday, the time to return, they had vanished. After some investigation, it was discovered he had taken the child to Thailand and had been there for about six months when they were located in Phuket.

With the father's name and passport information in hand, online research and calls revealed he was selling timeshares in Phuket, a job that's common for foreigners in Thailand. His daughter, who was about eight years old when she was kidnapped, was attending an international school there. The plan was to navigate the complex logistics of extracting both the father and daughter from Thailand, ensure they traveled back to America separately, and coordinate with the State Department for the child's care and the subsequent reunion with her mother.

In Phuket, the approach was delicate, requiring simultaneous action to avoid alarming the father or leaving the child stranded. We arranged two teams, one to apprehend the father and another to ensure the daughter was safely taken from her school.

But we had to adjust our plan on the fly. The father decided to visit his daughter at school on the same day we planned our operation. We had to ensure the child was found and secured before we approached the father so as to avoid him being tipped off and fleeing with his daughter.

When the father was arrested, he was understandably frantic about his daughter's welfare. Considering the emotional toll on the child, we decided to allow a brief reunion where the father could explain the situation to her, ensuring that she understood the next steps. This was a difficult moment for everyone involved. The father confessed his actions and expressed his reasons, painting a picture of his desperate attempt to protect his daughter from what he perceived as an unfit environment with her mother.

The deportation process was straightforward: the father and I spoke throughout the flight back to America. It was an encounter that left me feeling sympathetic for him. He was a former Marine and by all appearances a caring father, though his methods were undeniably flawed. Meanwhile, the daughter was safely escorted by a State Department official to reunite with her mother.

The case later took a frustrating turn. During the trial, the prosecution painted a misleading picture of Thailand as a war zone, using unrelated and outdated images to bolster their argument that the father took his daughter to a dangerous third-world country. This misrepresentation bothered me. It didn't accurately reflect the true nature of the father's actions or the environment the daughter had been living in.

But I didn't act on my feelings. My job was clear: locate the fugitive, work with the Embassy to make his passport revocable, arrange his deportation, fly him safely back to the US, and hand him over to the US agents. I knew he broke the law. He had other ways he could have addressed his frustrations with the child custody arrangement. Kidnapping his daughter was never going to be the right choice.

Despite the complexity of emotions surrounding the case, the fact remained clear: the father had kidnapped his daughter, violating custody agreements. During our discussion on the flight back to the US, the father suggested that he should have gone to China rather than fleeing to Thailand, a decision that ultimately led to a significant prison sentence. In China, he felt, he would have gotten away with it. His belief was that the Chinese government would not have been as quick to offer the investigative assistance Thailand provided.

When I heard that, any sympathy I had for him went out the window.

Fugitive case #3: the rapist

The phone rang late one evening; the voice on the other end belonged to an agent in Los Angeles—the Orange County FBI Office, to be more precise. She relayed a baffling story: many years ago, a man had raped his teenage daughter and fled to Thailand. Over the years, the trail had gone cold. The daughter, now likely in her 30s, had been just 17 at the time of the rape. It seemed as though the man had evaporated into thin air.

Then, unexpectedly, the fugitive reached out. He sent his daughter a letter, apparently believing enough time had elapsed to erase his trail. Remarkably, he included his return address in Thailand on the envelope.

"John," the agent exclaimed, "you're not going to believe this."

I was skeptical. "Just give me the address," I replied, "but let's not assume it will be this straightforward."

The first visit was just me and my ALAT, no one else. Our journey took us south of Bangkok, deep into the heart of Chonburi province, close to the city of Pattaya. We decided against notifying the Thai police, which in hindsight was a mistake, because we suspected it might be a fruitless chase.

Arriving at a gated community, we stationed ourselves outside a particular residence. Hours ticked by with little to show, only a Thai woman entering and leaving the home, raising questions about whether he still lived there. Just as we were on the verge of abandoning the stakeout, we opted to consult with the complex's manager, discreetly, given the unknowns about resident-manager relationships.

The manager wasn't around, so I glanced through the office window and spotted a map of the complex on the desk. Each house was labeled with names, and I was able to spot his name, in Thai, marked on the map.

A surge of adrenaline followed. "He's here. We've got him," I murmured under my breath.

I told the agent to fly out; I was certain it wasn't going to be a waste of time or money.

We refrained from immediate action, choosing instead to confirm our findings. After taking a photograph of the map, we left to plan the arrest with the US agent who had originally tipped us off.

A week or so later, we returned with the case agent. She was still jetlagged from her journey from the US but amped up for what she felt was to be the culmination of all of her hard work on this case. We were ready to execute the arrest. However, the target had moved, a planned departure he had set in motion over a month prior. We had confirmed this address only a week prior. We later found out he had lived in this house for almost 10 years. Our timing was just as unlucky as it gets.

I felt terrible. I'd been so confident, practically promising the agent, "We've got him." And then, just like that, he was gone.

The manager didn't have a forwarding address, and we thought we had lost him, but the story took another fortuitous turn. A gardener who was employed by the housing complex was approached by Thai police officers working with us on the case. The police showed the gardener a photograph of our fugitive to see if he recognized the man. Amazingly, the gardener had assisted the fugitive and his family with the move to their new house.

"Where to?" we pressed eagerly.

"Not far. Just five to 10 minutes away by car," he replied.

We followed the lead...and there he was. We arrested him without incident.

Before deportation, we allowed a brief goodbye between him, his new wife, and their son. En route back to the US, he was talkative, but unlike the parental kidnapper and Irish mobster, I had no desire to talk to him.

During my duties, I've come across all types. The Irish gangster was a notorious figure with stories from the Vietnam War. Despite his criminal background, I found myself intrigued by his tales. After all, I am an FBI agent, but also a human interested in gripping stories. The parental kidnapper was forthcoming about his experiences and motivations, which provided a humane glimpse into his actions, despite the circumstances. The rapist was talkative, too, but I couldn't see past his crime of child rape, so I had no interest in speaking with him.

I put my headphones on and watched a movie. Eventually, he fell asleep.

Handling dramatic moments

Occasionally, these flights offer dramatic moments, such as law enforcement boarding at LAX to detain someone, which can alarm unsuspecting fellow passengers. These situations sometimes lead to public interactions after the flight, where people express gratitude or concern. Explaining the safety measures and control maintained during these operations often reassures them, though concerns about flying with fugitives are not uncommon.

Such flights can unsettle passengers, who are surprised to find themselves in close quarters with a fugitive. Despite this, it's essential to manage the situation discreetly and ensure the safety of all onboard. The reality of transporting fugitives in this manner is a delicate balance of security and subtlety, a nuanced aspect of law enforcement that goes largely unseen by the public eye.

The importance of timing

In reflecting on these fugitive cases, it's evident that every second is crucial. Consider the instance of the Irish mobster. Our timely intervention caught him just as he was preparing to switch hotels. Had we arrived even a minute later, he might have vanished. Such scenarios underscore the critical nature of timing in our operations.

The case involving the parental kidnapping illustrates another instance of where timing played a crucial role. It wasn't a pursuit or a frantic chase; instead, it demanded perfectly synchronized actions. Arresting the father or securing the daughter prematurely could have led to turmoil or panic, akin to setting off a meticulously arranged row of dominoes where every piece must fall at precisely the right moment.

And then there's the case of the fugitive who, after 10 years at the same address, decided to move just as we were closing in. A week later, and he could have been anywhere, potentially even out of the country. Instead, he relocated merely 10 minutes away. This wasn't a calculated move on his part but rather fortuitous timing on ours, highlighting how serendipity can play as significant a role as strategy in our line of work.

Speaking of serendipity, without a dose of it, a major white-collar crime case in Bangkok might have turned out very differently.

CHAPTER 8

WHITE-COLLAR CRIME

BEING AN FBI AGENT ISN'T JUST A JOB; IT'S A 24/7 commitment.

And being overseas in Bangkok takes that aspect up a notch, because it's in a completely opposite time zone from the US.

When it's "quitting time" here, it's 3:00 or 4:00 p.m. in London, and DC is just waking up. When my office in Bangkok was open, FBI HQ in the States was closed. When Bangkok closed, HQ was starting the day.

Most nights, I'd come home around 8:00 p.m. and put down my BlackBerry, and as soon as I tried to relax, the emails started rolling in. By morning, there'd be a stack of them waiting. I kept my phone on for emergencies, which meant *10 years* of checking it every time it buzzed.

And more times than not, I'd get an email that started with: "I'm not sure what time it is over there, but..."

I always wanted to reply, "Buddy, it's called Google. Just type in 'what time is it in Thailand?'"

I never said it because it's part of the job. Every legat knows what they're signing up for. And I didn't want to start relationships that way. For a new agent stateside, I might be the first person they interact with in the International Operations Division, and it's my chance to show them what working with us is like.

Overseas, working 24/7 is a badge of honor. "I know it's 2:00 a.m. I'm sorry" is one thing when it's an emergency—I'm happy to help anytime—but when it isn't?

One particular case, a white-collar crime case involving a Nashville law firm, is a perfect example of an emergency that makes the time zone difference a non-issue and an example of a case when timing was everything. The email came in on a Friday night, at the end of a long work week, after most non-law enforcement officers were finished and heading into the weekend.

I worked on it all weekend.

Friday night

I remember this case like it was yesterday. I was at home around 7:30 p.m. on a Friday night when I got an email from Scott Augenbaum in the Memphis office (Memphis also covered Nashville at this time). The email was addressed to both me and my boss, but my boss was out of town, so I stepped in as the ALAT to handle it.

Scott was the supervisor of the cyber crime squad in the Memphis office. He was, and still is, well regarded in cyber fraud circles (he's actually written books on the topic, including *The Secret to Cybersecurity*). In his email, Scott explained that he'd been working with a Nashville law firm that had just fallen for a scam; the firm had wired out about $500,000 to an account in Thailand.

The law firm was approached by someone posing as an attorney from out of state, seeking representation for a foreign corporation in a debt collection against a local company. The law firm sent a demand letter on behalf of their new client and soon received a check from the debtor. They deposited this check into their trust account and wired the funds, minus their fees, to the client's bank account overseas. The situation unraveled when the bank alerted them that the check was counterfeit, but by then the wire transfer was irreversible. Scott knew it was late Friday night in Thailand and wasn't sure how much we could do from our end, but he hoped that since it was still Friday morning in the US, maybe the transfer hadn't fully processed yet, and there was still time to act.

But he also knew it was a long shot. He pointed out that often with cyber fraud schemes, the funds *are* transferred out almost instantly through an automatic withdrawal in the fraudster's foreign bank account. So there was a very real chance the money was already gone by the time I was reading his email.

In the United States, most fraud losses remain unrecovered; federal law enforcement sometimes has success when they respond rapidly, but only 43% of occupational fraud cases yield any financial recovery, with just 13% fully compensating victims.[7] This low recovery rate highlights the difficulty in tracking funds after they've been transferred, especially when fraudsters employ swift, sophisticated transfer techniques across multiple accounts or offshore locations. By the time victims report the crime, fraudsters have often moved the money quickly out of accessible channels.

Globally, asset recovery becomes even more complex. International fraudsters commonly use layered transactions and offshore accounts to make funds inaccessible. In fact, in 2018, less than 1% of the $110B of criminal restitution ordered by the US DOJ was recovered due to jurisdictional and logistical barriers.[8]

And in Thailand, where many international scams are routed, recoveries are rare and generally require extensive cooperation between local banks and law enforcement agencies. While Thai authorities can sometimes freeze accounts if they act quickly, international banking laws and proce-

---

7   Association of Certified Fraud Examiners, *2020 Report to the Nations: Banking and Financial Services Edition* (ACFE, 2020).

8   US Government Accountability Office, *Federal Prison System: Justice Could Better Analyze Staffing Data to Improve Employee Allocation Decisions* (GAO, 2018).

dural delays often make it difficult to retrieve money once it's transferred out of the country.

I called immediately to let Scott know I'd received his message, and while I assured him I'd do what I could, I also wanted to manage expectations based on my experience. When money is wired internationally, it's incredibly hard to track and recover. This was by far the largest amount I'd dealt with, and the structure of the scam (more on this in a moment) made the likelihood of getting the money back very low. The better the scammer, the faster that money leaves the account.

When this case came up in May of 2009, bank fraud was common in Thailand. Just about anyone could open a bank account. And the public's knowledge of fraud was limited.

These days, it's tougher to get fooled by the old-school scams because it's pretty easy to check if someone is legit with tools like Zoom and other chat apps. But even with better security and smarter cops, the bad guys are always finding new ways to rip people off.

Today, anyone can visit the FBI's website and learn about the most common fraud types in the US and abroad.

There are also a lot of people in Thailand (tourists) who are susceptible to fraud.

I'd only been there for a few months (since December of 2008), so I was about five months into my assignment. Even with that limited time, I'd already seen a couple of cases, and in every single one, the money was always gone before we could get our hands on it. This particular law firm, though, figured out pretty early on that it was a scam.

On the phone with Scott, I was standing in my bedroom, juggling my phone and a notepad, jotting down details. I didn't have a home office, so I hunched over and wrote on a book on my bed.

The fraudsters demonstrated their ability to manipulate the transaction when they redirected the payment destination at the last minute: "Actually, use our Bangkok account instead." So the funds were sent to the Bangkok account, intended for immediate withdrawal. My job was to see if there was any chance to intercept the funds before they disappeared completely. Scott asked me to get in touch with the bank and law firm directly to try to salvage what we could.

It was already past 8:00 p.m., and there was no way the bank would be open.

"Here's the plan. It's too late to contact the bank tonight. I'll try to locate it first thing tomorrow and then reach out to my contacts in the Thai police."

I took the lead early on, and Scott approved. I kept him in copy on all communication and updated him regularly.

After my call with Scott, I contacted the law firm, relayed the plan, and said, "I hate to say it, but I have a gut feeling the money's already gone."

Scott had already done a good job of managing expectations, so the lawyer wasn't shocked to hear this.

Still, we hung on the hope that there was a chance. It was Friday, so maybe we'd get lucky.

That night, I hardly slept, thinking over the strategy. At five months in, I still had that new-agent optimism. A veteran might have said, "There's no way," but I thought, *I can pull this off*.

I decided to wait to call my Thai police contacts until I had solid information. All I had was a possible bank location (I wasn't even sure it existed), and I decided to confirm the details in the morning. By then, I'd been on calls with agents in Memphis and the firm's contact in Nashville, and it was nearing 10:00 p.m. I'd pick the work back up the next morning.

Saturday morning

Saturday morning rolled around, and no surprise, I was up early. My son was around three at the time, so we had some kind of kid activity lined up, probably a swim lesson or soccer practice. It could've been a birthday party. I remembered needing to be somewhere and watching him while fielding phone calls.

Multitasking at its finest.

The first thing I did, around 10:00 a.m. when the banks opened, was verify that this particular bank actually existed. I went online and punched in the address, and sure enough, it was there. The bank was Kasikorn Bank, known as K Bank, one of the biggest around, think Bank of America in the States. The branch we needed to visit was in a heavily trafficked area, packed with offices and businesses, in a bustling part of Bangkok.

In Thailand, I'd already learned that whenever you needed to do anything bank-related, you had to show up in person. It was the same for my personal banking.

As Bangkok Bank members, whenever my wife or I needed to get something done, we had to go in person to our branch. That's just how it is with banking in Thailand: everything's very hands-on at the branch level.

But being the naive optimist I was, I thought, *Why not just call the bank?*

I dialed Kasikorn Bank, fully expecting that it would go nowhere. Surprisingly, someone picked up. (An advantage in Thailand is that customer service is available on Saturdays.) I pressed the number for English, since my Thai was decent but not quite up to handling this kind of request.

"You're not going to believe this, but I'm an FBI agent," I told the person on the other end.

Imagine being a Thai customer service rep and hearing that out of nowhere. An American FBI agent calling you up.

I explained, "I work at the US Embassy, and I'm investigating a case where someone in America was defrauded. They transferred approximately $500,000 to your bank branch in Bangkok. I don't expect you to simply hand over information, but if I give you the account number, can you just tell me if the money is still in there? I don't need access or details. Just whether it's still sitting in the account."

I went on to assure him, "You can verify my identity if you want. You can call back to the embassy and ask for the FBI agent, John, at this number. It's all legit."

Throughout all this, I thought, *There's no way he'll actually do this for me.*

But he said, "Hold on a second."

I waited, fully expecting him to come back with a polite refusal, but instead, he said, "Sir, an amount equivalent to what you mentioned is still in the account."

I was floored. "You are the greatest person ever," I told him. "Thank you so much. I really appreciate it."

I thought, *All right, maybe we've got something here.*

I was still fielding calls while watching my son at one of his many weekend activities when the money was confirmed to be in the account. It was around 10:00 a.m. in Bangkok, which made it about 9:00 or 10:00 p.m. in Tennessee.

First, I called Scott in Memphis and told him, "Don't get your hopes up. This doesn't mean we're getting the money back, just that we've got a shot."

It was possible that the funds could transfer automatically, before I had a chance to intercept.

Next up: the attorney who lost approximately $500K of the firm's money.

It was late, but the night before, I'd spoken to him when he was beside himself, thinking his job was on the line. He'd told me, "John, you can call me anytime."

So I called him to let him know the money was still in the account but that nothing was guaranteed. We hadn't won yet.

He was so relieved and excited; you could practically hear him exhale.

Saturday afternoon

I hung up with the agent and attorney after giving them the good news, then called my Thai police contact at the time, Sinard (I hadn't met my good friend, Aod, yet). I said, "Here's the deal. I need to meet you for lunch." Now, explaining this financial crime case was a bit tricky; it wasn't the typical kind of crime they dealt with, especially back in 2009, when financial crimes weren't as big in Thailand. And Sinard wasn't from a financial crimes unit; he was just a cop I trusted and knew could help.

At that point, I thought, *Okay, what's the plan?*

With no real experience handling a case like this in Thailand, I came up with an idea. I figured we'd head to the bank first thing Monday morning. I checked online, and the bank opened at 8:00 a.m.

"Let's get there at 7:45, 7:50, and see who shows up. No one's taking $500K out of an ATM, so we might catch someone in person," I told my colleague.

We later met for a beer, as you do in Thailand.

In Bangkok, bars come in all flavors, from familiar no-smoking zones like those in the States to dives and upscale lounges that pack their own style. But my favorite, and the choice that day, is the roadside bar. I'm talking plastic tables with cold beers on the sidewalk, smack in the middle of traffic noise, wearing your shorts, T-shirt, and sneakers, much more casual than the office's suit and tie or the khakis and polo that I later wore to the bank.

This bar was reasonably full—not packed, but not empty either.

Over drinks, I laid out my plan, and he was on board.

Sinard brought in another contact and mutual friend to both of us, Colonel Udon. Sinard and Udon were two of my closest contacts, both FBI National Academy graduates (Sindard is now retired, and Udon is a General). Udon wasn't at the in-person meeting, but when I later explained the details of the fraud and how the law firm got scammed, he agreed and was ready to back up Sinard and me.

By Saturday afternoon, we had a plan.

Sunday morning

All this time, the Memphis office and the Nashville law firm were trying to pull the money back.

You might be thinking, *If the money's still there, why can't they go to the bank and say, "Hey, this was a fraudulent check. Give it back?"*

International banking law doesn't work that way. I learned a lot about that in this case.

As I tracked emails between the law firm and the bank, I saw the firm was trying every option to reverse the check. I was copied on every internal discussion, and it was eye-opening to see just how difficult it was to pull funds back internationally.

Once you send money, it's mostly a done deal. The check cleared, and as far as the bank was concerned, it was legitimate.

These fraudsters knew what they were doing. They used a CitiBank check for the front, and the local Nashville bank followed standard procedure to verify it. There's a verification line banks call to confirm checks, and somehow, this one passed the test.

So the money got transferred. All weekend, the law firm tried to reverse it but couldn't. K Bank even has a branch in Los Angeles, and they tried through that office, too, but no luck.

On Sunday, I got the call confirming the transfer couldn't be reversed.

I spent the rest of the day getting my things ready for Monday morning.

Monday morning

Monday morning, we were ready to go. I wanted to get to the bank about 10–15 minutes early. We arrived, waited outside, and went in as soon as it opened.

It was like a typical bank branch you'd find tucked inside a shopping mall or Walmart, standalone but small. There were two teller stations, less than 10 chairs in the waiting area, and a couple of manager offices in the back. It was already crowded when we arrived; eight out of 10 chairs were full, and people were waiting. Nothing unusual, just a busy, tight-knit setup.

We kept it low-key: no FBI gear or suits, and my colleagues weren't in any Royal Thai Police attire either. We didn't know who else might be watching.

We quietly pulled the bank manager aside, and he told us, "Funny you're here right now. There are two African men sitting in the waiting room. They came here on Friday night to withdraw money from the account in question but forgot their bank book."

And here they were on Monday, back to try again.

Because we showed up early, we were able to confront them on the spot.

We asked the bank manager to escort them to the back of the bank, where we were waiting for them.

As soon as we questioned them, they played innocent, acting shocked at even the hint that they were doing anything illegal. They claimed they were there to pick up money for a jewelry exchange.

"The money's from a jeweler back home," they said, "and we're here to complete the purchase."

Not exactly an admission of guilt, but from the start, it was clear that these guys were seasoned fraudsters. They never demanded their money or even asked for it. Despite their denials, at the end, they quickly agreed to drop it without a fight.

That reaction spoke volumes. If the money had been legitimate, they would have pushed back and argued to keep it. But their willingness to give it up so easily was essentially an unspoken admission of guilt. They didn't even try the classic line: "My boss is going to kill me." Instead, they just wanted to get out of there. Once they realized they weren't going to prison for life, they were all too happy to let the money go, which pretty much screamed guilt to me.

Turned out, they were in Thailand illegally, so the Thai police were left to decide what to do with them. At the end of the day, it was an American fraud case, and all we cared about was recovering the funds.

In the US, white-collar crime cases are often based on financial loss, and since we recovered the funds, technically, there was no loss to pursue. In this instance, the FBI decided it wasn't worth spending resources on extradition for them. Our focus was on getting the money back, which we eventually did, though it took a few months due to international banking regulations.

My recommendation was straightforward: deport the two fraudsters. The RTP ended up taking that advice.

The aftermath

Scott was 100% thankful and appreciative, nothing but professional and courteous throughout. We even connected on LinkedIn and kept in touch over the years, exchanging the occasional hello. He was a phenomenal agent, and we had a great rapport. I received a lot of positive feedback, praise, and thanks from him, which meant a lot.

The way cases like this play out in movies is far from reality. In shows, they often hit a moment where the suspect admits guilt or jots down a confession. But in real life, it's not that simple. Often, there are no admissions or confessions, and getting to the truth requires a lot of investigative work.

Recovering those funds was a major win. It's one thing to call the LAPD if you lose money to someone in LA; even then, you'd probably never see it again. But here, Nashville had to call Memphis, and Memphis reached out to the FBI in Bangkok. And somehow, we got it back.

In all my time in law enforcement, I've yet to meet anyone else, FBI, RTP, you name it, who has managed to bring anything back, let alone approximately $500K. I was able to call the lawyer, who was fully convinced he was about to be fired. When I told him the money was recovered, he was beyond grateful.

I later found out that he kept his job.

It took months for the law firm to finally recover the funds through a lengthy civil procedure. Although I wasn't directly involved in this part, it was a drawn-out process, typical of international cases like this. But in the end, they got their money back.

But it wasn't just recovering the money that made me feel good. The whole process made this one of the most satisfying cases of my career.

This case was one of the highlights of my time in Bangkok, but my duties stretched beyond Thailand's borders, reaching the countries of Laos and Myanmar as well.

CHAPTER 9

LAOS AND MYANMAR

AS PART OF MY ROLE WITH THE FBI, I DIDN'T JUST cover cases in Thailand; my jurisdiction extended to neighboring countries too. This included Laos and Myanmar, each with its own set of unique challenges and intriguing stories.

Myanmar is currently a global focal point due to ongoing conflicts, making it a hot-button topic, but my experiences there and in Laos have been particularly memorable for different reasons; in Laos, I helped hunt for one of the FBI's top 10 fugitives, who was supposedly spotted while President Obama was on an official visit.

Myanmar was a unique challenge. During my first tour as the ALAT, getting in was nearly impossible. They kept denying our visa applications, likely suspecting us of being intelligence officers (CIA), which made them suspicious. They didn't know we were the FBI and were there to *help* them.

But while I was back in the US between tours, things shifted. In 2013, a bomb went off in a hotel in Myanmar, injuring an American citizen, and that incident opened the door for our involvement. My predecessor handled the initial request, but when I returned as the legat, I made it my mission to build on that progress.

I took my first trip to Myanmar early in my second tour and met with the Chief of the Myanmar Police Force (MPF) and his top deputies. The history of the police force was eye-opening. Years of political turmoil had led the military-backed government to disband the old police force and rebuild it using military personnel. The result was a force lacking even basic police training.

I knew that telling them they needed my help because they weren't advanced wouldn't go over well. So I took a different approach: I told them I was there to help protect

Myanmar from "bad Americans." At the time, Myanmar was starting to open up to the West, with stories of American businesses and tourists flocking there. (More on Myanmar's history a bit later.) I explained to the Chief that while some Americans would be there to do good, others might bring problems like corruption and child exploitation. My pitch was simple: "I'm here to help you keep the bad ones out."

It worked. Over the next few months, I made multiple trips, teaching classes to the police and assisting on a few cases of mutual interest. It felt like we were making real progress.

But as I write this, it's disheartening to see those gains vanish. Political turmoil has flared up in Myanmar again, and the bridges we built have all but closed, taking the US back to square one.

And with a massive earthquake hitting Myanmar on March 28, 2025, Myanmar is once again in need of international assistance, something they seem to unfortunately shy away from.

My involvement wasn't needed too often in either country. While I was in Bangkok, I visited Laos three times and Myanmar four.

These experiences underline not just the complexity of the regions but also the unpredictable nature of my work across these two fascinating countries.

Laos

Laos has a strong French colonial resemblance; you can see it in everything from their legal system to how the bureaucracy runs. It's a noticeable contrast to Myanmar, which has more of a British colonial influence baked into its systems.

The way Laos approaches law enforcement and administration still has that French flavor, which makes it feel very different from a lot of its neighbors in the region.

But it's not just about the French influence. Laos is also heavily shaped by its neighbors; Vietnam, China, and Japan all play big roles in the country's development. Vietnam and China, in particular, have a lot of sway due to their proximity and historical connections with Laos. Their influence is clear in many areas, from economics to politics to social dynamics, making them key players in how Laos interacts with the rest of the world and manages its internal affairs.

Japan's role is a bit different. It's not about direct governance but more about development aid and cultural exchange. Japanese NGOs are pretty active in Laos, working on projects that support local development. This has strengthened the ties between the two countries, particularly in terms of cultural and economic relationships. All these influences come together to create a unique blend of cultural dynamics in Laos, setting it apart from other Southeast Asian nations and giving it a character that's neither purely Western nor entirely like its neighbors.

Law enforcement

During my time in Laos, I ran into an interesting attitude from the local officials. They were pretty skeptical about needing help from the FBI. They actually claimed, quite boldly, that there was no crime in Laos. I couldn't help but find that a bit amusing and, to be honest, a little naive. It really showed just how different our perspectives on crime and law enforcement were.

In one training session with the Laotian police officers, I

was explaining the standard FBI procedure after a suspect confesses. In the US, even if someone admits to a crime, we don't just stop there. We keep investigating to make sure everything lines up. We verify the suspect's whereabouts at the time, confirm details at the crime scene, and match physical evidence to the confession. It's about making sure every aspect of the crime is thoroughly documented and verified.

But as I was going through this, I noticed some puzzled looks from the officers. One of them raised his hand and, with genuine confusion, asked why we'd keep investigating if the suspect had already admitted guilt. To them, once a confession was made, the investigation was over. That was it. This question really hit home just how differently we approach things. In Laos, a confession seemed to be the end of the road, which to me felt like a premature conclusion.

I tried to explain again why it's important to back up the confession with evidence. It's about ensuring the integrity of the conviction and protecting against false confessions. But then another officer chimed in, still not understanding why we'd go any further once someone had confessed. This whole exchange highlighted a fundamental challenge in working across different legal systems. There was a real gap between our judicial philosophies and investigative techniques. It was a clear reminder of how deeply cultural norms and historical practices influence the way law enforcement operates and how justice is delivered in different parts of the world.

A visit from President Obama

During President Obama's visit to Laos in 2016, something unexpected happened that pulled both the Secret Service and the FBI into action. A Secret Service agent who was part of the president's detail thought he spotted someone who looked like one of the FBI's top 10 fugitives. The agent waited until he returned from the presidential visit to contact the FBI to report the potential sighting. His information provided us with two areas in the Laos city of Luang Prabang where he believed the fugitive sighting happened, but that was the extent of what we had to go with. Given the seriousness of the situation, this report triggered a swift and coordinated response from the FBI. The idea that a top fugitive could be nearby during such a high-profile event meant we had to act immediately.

After President Obama left Laos, I traveled to Luang Prabang with my ALAT, Ernie Weyand, to investigate the sighting. The stakes were high, not only because of the president's presence but also because of what it would mean if a dangerous fugitive was actually in the area. My response was carefully planned. I needed to verify the sighting without causing unnecessary alarm or interfering with the ongoing diplomatic activities after the president's visit.

On-the-ground investigations like this are a key part of how the FBI handles reports of top-10 fugitive sightings, especially when they involve international travel and the presence of US dignitaries.

Fluent in English

I positioned myself in one of the areas from the tip provided by the Secret Service Agent. Luckily, there was a local pub with outside seating that provided a good view of the general area. I entered the pub and decided that a quick conversation with the Western-looking bar owner may help, as local pubs can be a meeting spot for expats in small communities like the one I was in.

I showed the photo of the fugitive to the owner, and to my surprise, he said he recognized the man. The most recent photo we had was many years old, so he wasn't sure of his identification, but he was confident the man lived in the area because he walked by his pub frequently. This was very good information and gave me a small bit of encouragement that this may not be a wasted effort. I had convinced myself that the man the Secret Service Agent saw was a tourist who had left Laos for good.

I asked Ernie to stake out the other area of the city where the Secret Service agent thought the fugitive might be, even though the bar owner's tip made me think I was in a better spot.

Around 9:00 a.m., I took a seat outside the bar, ordered breakfast as a thank-you for letting me use the place for surveillance, and settled in, still expecting a long three days before heading back to Bangkok empty-handed.

To my surprise, less than an hour later, as a few people passed by, a man walked up the road toward the bar. The owner rushed over and pointed him out as the guy he had mentioned earlier.

I approached the man slowly, trying not to startle him, and asked if I could speak with him for a moment. His response came with a clear British accent, which immediately told me he wasn't our guy; the fugitive we were looking for was an American. Now, the question was whether this was the person the Secret Service agent had spotted. I identified myself as an FBI agent and asked for his ID, making sure he understood he wasn't obligated to stay. I reassured him that as a British citizen with a valid passport, he wasn't who we were searching for, but I needed to close the loop.

I contacted the Secret Service agent, who I had asked to stay on standby for three days while we pursued this lead. He picked up, and when I sent him a photo of the man, he immediately confirmed (with 100% certainty) that this was the person he had mentioned in his initial call. With that, we were able to close out the lead. The British man, who had kindly stuck around, remarked that this was the coolest thing that had ever happened to him.

To be clear, the FBI did not work with the Laotian police on this case. Well, not officially. We worked with our US Embassy law enforcement partners, who had a better working relationship with the Laos police. They worked with the Laos government more than we did, sitting in Bangkok. Our Embassy colleagues told me that getting approval for the FBI to work a fugitive matter, like what we had, would take weeks, not days. And we just didn't have the time to wait.

Sometimes, the sensitivity of these kinds of operations means things happen with a sort of "wink and a nod," like in this case. While our two governments might not always see eye to eye, sometimes even showing a bit of animosity, especially when Laos aligns more closely with political rivals like China or Vietnam, it's always good to see law enforcement find ways to cooperate. The Laos police knew letting the FBI openly work a case would be a tough ask, so we were told they were happy accepting our written request, and they would keep one eye closed as we went about our business.

Clear as mud?

Yeah, that was what we thought. But sometimes that's the best you can hope for.

Fast and clear communication

The case of the suspected sighting of a top-10 fugitive during President Obama's visit to Laos brought out one of the challenges that comes with international law enforcement cooperation. It showed just how tricky it can be when US agencies like the FBI have to operate within the legal and procedural frameworks of a foreign country without any help from local authorities.

Another big challenge we faced was dealing with the differences in legal systems and investigative procedures. In Laos, as in many other countries with unique legal traditions, the local laws and law enforcement practices don't always line up with what we're used to in the US. This can cause misunderstandings and delays, which are especially problematic in high-pressure situations where public safety and the security of diplomatic figures are at stake.

On top of that, the situation proved the need for cultural sensitivity and the ability to quickly adapt to local customs and expectations without losing sight of the mission's objectives. Ernie and I had to be very culturally aware and to make sure we were respecting local norms.

We had to keep a low profile. Between the expat bar owner and the expat who might have been a top-10 fugitive, we were in a delicate position. As foreigners, we were essentially guests in the country, operating under the radar. It was important not to draw attention to ourselves or create any diplomatic waves. We had to respect the wishes of our Laotian counterparts in law enforcement and ensure that none of our actions would come back to cause problems for them with their superiors. It was all about finding a balance, doing our job without rocking the boat.

This incident was a real test of the FBI's operational

capabilities in an international setting. It pinpointed just how important strong international partnerships and mutual understanding are when it comes to global law enforcement efforts.

I didn't end up doing much in Laos after that. The only other case we handled that involved Laos was the murder of a US citizen. It was a particularly violent death, and there was a lot of blood spread all over the house. It was later confirmed that the victim died of blunt force trauma. Ernie Weyand had a wealth of experience with murder investigations, so the US Embassy in Vientiane asked him to step in and assist.

Ernie did everything he could, but the case was bogged down by roadblocks and bureaucratic hurdles. Every step forward seemed to come with a new setback. Ultimately, our role in the case came to an end, and we had to walk away without a resolution that would meet our standards for justice. It was a tough pill to swallow, knowing we couldn't bring closure to that case.

Myanmar

Myanmar used to be known as Burma.

It's one of those countries you want to work in until you get there and realize just how complicated things really are. When I first traveled to Myanmar, there was this brief window of hope: democratic elections had just taken place. Aung San Suu Kyi was in power, and US businesses were gearing up to invest. I mean, everyone from Coca-Cola to major hotel chains was ready to pounce. Myanmar, with its natural beauty and sheer size, seemed poised to become Southeast Asia's next success story.

That optimism didn't last.

Today, Myanmar is right back in chaos. Aung San Suu Kyi is once again in custody. The military has taken control, and the country is locked in what amounts to a violent political crisis—maybe not quite a civil war, but certainly not a stable democracy. The US government is trying to push for reforms at the highest diplomatic levels, but from where I sit (and from what I've seen), there just isn't a strong enough reason for the FBI to push its way in right now.

And that's the tricky part. You can't do meaningful law enforcement work in a country where the government's overwhelmed, hostile to outsiders, or simply uninterested. Even when I was there during the "good" years, there weren't a lot of cases to work. But I still saw value. I went to Myanmar to build capacity and help local law enforcement prepare for what we thought would be an influx of Americans.

And when you open a country's doors to US business and tourism, you'd better make sure their police are ready. That was my mission.

I ran trainings. I met officers who were eager to learn. I loved it. But history and Myanmar's political reality keep getting in the way. The current legat in Bangkok is probably itching to do more there, just like I was. But unless something changes dramatically, Myanmar will continue to be a tough place for any real FBI presence.

Coup after coup after coup

Myanmar's political history has been marked by a series of military coups since its independence from Britain in the 1940s. This has resulted in long stretches of military rule. This cycle of military takeovers has kept the country politically cut off from the rest of the world and heavily influenced how the country has run things, both at home and abroad.

After gaining independence, Myanmar had a tough time transitioning into a stable democracy. Instead, the military maintained control for decades, making things even messier, with constant ethnic tension and unrest as different groups fought for power or independence. These conflicts often turned violent, making the situation even more complex.

This messy history has left a lasting impact on Myanmar's development, international relations, and the daily lives of its citizens. Even today, the nation continues to navigate the tensions between military influence and the push for democratic reforms.

Limited FBI engagement

Political instability in Myanmar, especially during military coups, made it tough for the FBI to operate there. With all the chaos and shifting leadership, it was nearly impossible to build the kind of steady, reliable partnerships we need to do effective law enforcement work.

The US embassy also hit roadblocks during these times. Ongoing turmoil made it hard to carry out basic diplomatic and law enforcement coordination, which meant the FBI couldn't fully engage, whether that was running investigations, gathering intel, or helping train and support local police.

All of this didn't just affect the FBI. It also slowed down international aid, development projects, and broader security efforts...basically everything that would help Myanmar stay connected to the global community.

Aung San Suu Kyi

Things started to shift when Aung San Suu Kyi, a well-known political activist and leader of the National League for Democracy, was released from house arrest and later elected to office. After years under military rule, her rise symbolized what many hoped would be a real step toward democracy. It was a turning point that signaled change might finally be possible.

Following her release, Aung San Suu Kyi's election to office marked a significant change in how the international community, particularly the United States, engaged with Myanmar. This period also coincided with the US officially recognizing the country by its self-identified name, Myanmar, moving away from the colonial-era name, Burma. The name change mattered: it was a way of formally recognizing the country's sovereignty and signaling a move toward respecting its right to shape its own path.

The change in relations was not just symbolic but also practical. Diplomatic interactions (including FBI involvement) increased, and some international sanctions were eased. There was a boost in foreign aid and investment, all aimed at supporting Myanmar's march toward democratization. The US and other nations saw Aung San Suu Kyi's leadership as an opportunity to support reforms that could lead to more stable and democratic governance in Myanmar.

Myanmar was opening up to the world…and the world was welcoming it with open arms.

The FBI's approach

As Myanmar began to open its doors to the world, the FBI recognized both the challenges and opportunities that came with this transition. As the country started opening up to tourism and foreign business, it seemed full of potential: like real economic growth and global partnerships might finally be on the table. But it also exposed Myanmar to new risks, particularly in the realms of corruption and exploitation.

With the influx of outsiders came the risk of people with bad intentions exploiting the country's resources and its people. That kind of thing tends to happen in places where tourism is growing fast but the laws, systems, and law enforcement haven't quite caught up. It wasn't just about individual crimes; it was about the bigger picture and what this could mean for Myanmar's social fabric and international standing.

Myanmar's police force faced challenges because it was mostly made up of military personnel reassigned to police roles. While disciplined, they often lacked the specialized training needed for effective civilian law enforcement, especially in areas like community policing and investigations.

To address this, the FBI provided training programs aimed at bridging these gaps, introducing modern policing techniques and fostering respect for human rights. The Myanmar police showed a strong willingness to learn, recognizing the need for professional growth. The FBI's efforts helped equip them with skills in forensic analysis, crime scene management, and understanding civilian law, key elements for building trust and adapting to a more civilian-focused approach.

The FBI's involvement was all about helping Myanmar's police force deal with new threats. Our goal was to make sure Myanmar could not only manage but also control the risks that come with more foreign presence and help the country develop safely and sustainably.

These efforts were all about finding the right balance.

Myanmar was eager to jump on the economic opportunities that came with opening up to the world—but with that openness came new risks. More global exposure meant more potential for bad actors to slip in, and the country needed to figure out how to protect itself. As the country navigated this tricky path, partnerships with international law enforcement agencies like the FBI were crucial. We wanted to ensure Myanmar could make the most of its opportunities while keeping its citizens safe and protecting its cultural heritage from potential harm.

Public corruption

The FBI tailored our training programs to fit the country's specific needs.

One of the big concerns was public corruption. As Myanmar started to attract more foreign investment, the risk of corrupt practices increased, not just among local officials but also from international actors. Our training emphasized the importance of transparency and accountability. We made sure to teach the local police how to detect and fight corruption, which was crucial for helping Myanmar build a more stable and ethical business environment.

I taught a class on corruption, which included meeting with the Chief of Police and his top deputies. He even took me out to a restaurant in the almost-empty city of Naypyidaw, a surreal VIP experience (more on Naypyidaw later). They closed down a four-story restaurant just for us, and we spent a few hours over Chinese food and whiskey. It felt like one of those pinch-yourself moments. But those kinds of nights help secure training approvals and open doors for future collaborations.

Vulnerable population exploitation

Another critical focus for us was protecting vulnerable populations, especially children, from exploitation. With the expected rise in tourism, there was a real danger of Myanmar becoming a target for child sex tourism, a problem that has affected other Southeast Asian countries. We provided specialized training to help Myanmar's police spot and prevent this kind of exploitation. This included teaching them investigative techniques to track down and arrest offenders, as well as strategies for protecting victims and helping them recover.

The FBI's proactive stance in Myanmar wasn't just about tackling the immediate issues at hand. We were also looking ahead, preparing the country for the long-term challenges that come with integrating into the global community. Helping strengthen local law enforcement was one way we tried to support Myanmar through its growing pains, making sure that as the country opened up, it could stay both secure and on a steady path forward.

Capital relocation

One of the most puzzling events in Myanmar's recent history is the sudden decision in 2006 to relocate the capital from Yangon to Naypyidaw. This move, orchestrated by the military government, was carried out with little to no public explanation, leaving many to speculate about the true reasons behind it.

Naypyidaw, a city built from scratch in the middle of the country, was established in a cloak of secrecy. The reasons for the relocation remain murky, but several theories have been floated. Some suggest that the decision was driven by strategic military considerations. By moving the capital inland, far from the densely populated and historically significant Yangon, the government might have been seeking to better protect the seat of power from potential invasions or uprisings. The choice of Naypyidaw, in a more remote and defensible area, could have been seen as a way to maintain tighter control over the country.

Another theory is that the move was influenced by superstition or astrological advice. It's been rumored that military leaders, perhaps guided by astrologers or fortune tellers, believed that relocating the capital would shield the regime from external threats or align the nation's fate with more favorable outcomes. This mix of superstition and statecraft isn't unheard of in the region, where traditional beliefs often play a role in political decisions.

The decision to relocate the capital to Naypyidaw remains one of the weirdest choices in Myanmar's history. The whole thing just added to the mystery of how Myanmar operates. No one really knows if the decision was political, superstitious, or something else entirely, but whatever the reason, it definitely kept people guessing, both inside the country and out. The FBI had no involvement in the capital relocation. But the aftermath was hard to miss. Traveling there was an eye-opening experience, like what I imagine visiting North Korea would be like. Massive hotels with 300 rooms but only four guests. Huge highways without a single car in sight. It felt like a city built for show, not for people.

New tools and knowledge

The response to our training in Myanmar was overwhelmingly positive. The local police weren't just interested in gaining new knowledge; they were genuinely enthusiastic about applying these new skills to improve their capacity to serve and protect their communities more effectively and ethically. Their enthusiasm showed a strong commitment to bettering themselves and the way they operated.

But the training also showed us just how tough it is to shift a police force from a military-style mindset to one that actually serves the people in a democratic way. It wasn't just about teaching them how to run an investigation or process a crime scene. It was about changing the whole culture. We had to get them thinking in terms of accountability, transparency, and basic human rights. That's not a quick fix.

Was this effective? I'd say the jury's still out. It's tough for any international organization to access enough information to give a solid analysis of whether it's been effective. The limited transparency and restricted access make it hard to gauge the full impact or success of these efforts.

Were our efforts successful? Success in Myanmar when I was there looked very different than in other places, like Thailand. When I was Legat Bangkok, training sessions were routine, so we measured success by the impact, improved knowledge, more effective cases, arrests, and competent assistance with FBI operations. But in Myanmar, just being invited to teach was a win.

Success meant having open discussions about their legal system, fostering honest dialogue, getting them to accept FBI methods, and sharing intelligence. I even managed to establish the first-ever intel-sharing program between the FBI and Myanmar. I'd send them our FBI intel bulletins, and they'd reciprocate with insights from their side. A huge milestone.

In the end, the local police's eagerness for training

highlighted both the challenges they faced and their determination to overcome these obstacles. The FBI's assistance played a key role in this process, helping to equip Myanmar's police with the capabilities they needed.

While Myanmar and Laos were still bringing their law enforcement capabilities up to an international standard, a case I was assigned to in Bangkok would test even the most seasoned police officer, and it would also be the most interesting and satisfying of my entire career.

CHAPTER 10

BODY PARTS

ONE OF THE MOST DAUNTING AND DISTURBING CASES from my tenure began with a grotesque discovery in Bangkok: a human body, dismembered and meticulously preserved within the cold confines of a heavy-duty freezer.

It was a typical Friday afternoon on September 23, 2016. I had just left work and was on my way to pick up my son, who was then 10, from a playdate. He was at a friend's house, enjoying the afternoon with a few classmates from his international school. When I arrived to collect him, I was welcomed into the dining room by his friend's parents. They kindly offered me a drink to enjoy the end of the work week. Perhaps it was a beer, though I can't recall if I even opened it. As I was settling in, my phone—or more precisely, my messaging app—suddenly rang.

Communication in Thailand primarily happens through a messaging app called Line, a service developed by a Japanese company. Unlike other places where WhatsApp might dominate, Line is the preferred method here. Aod (who was also my closest Thai police partner), contacted me through Line, and his message was urgent. He relayed that during a police raid, an officer had been shot. He was expected to recover, but the raid had uncovered more than just the immediate danger. In the aftermath of the shooting, the team found a collection of passports from various countries, including a few from the US.

Aod asked for my help to verify the authenticity of these passports with the embassy. I agreed without hesitation and told him to send the photos of the passports. However, there was a brief delay, about five or 10 minutes, before Aod called back, instructing me to hold off, as the situation at the scene was still evolving.

When he called a third time, he had a more disturbing

update. The search had revealed what appeared to be parts of a dismembered, frozen body. The exact details were still unclear.

A collection of passports

When the Royal Thai Police, Tourist Police Bureau stopped a man in a tourist-heavy area of Bangkok on a sweltering day and asked for his passport, they had no idea it would lead them to a dismembered body.

Upon routine investigation, they discovered the passport was fraudulent, and when prompted, the man gave the police the address where he obtained it.

Naturally, the Thai police went to the location provided: a home on the outskirts of downtown Bangkok. When they approached the house identified during their initial investigation, a Western-looking man answered the door and was asked for identification. He told the police his passport was upstairs. The officers followed him to his room, where he claimed it was in a safe. However, instead of retrieving his passport, he suddenly pulled out a gun and turned to shoot at the officers, injuring one.

As soon as he shot at the RTP, they tackled and disarmed him before he could shoot anyone else.

They then searched the home and immediately, they found drugs, methamphetamine and marijuana.

They also found a lot more.

After the RTP officer was shot (the injured officer received prompt medical attention at the scene and was soon transported to a hospital for further treatment, thankfully with injuries that were not life-threatening), the team swiftly secured the area to prevent further violence, or any attempts by the other suspects detained at the scene to escape, and continued their search of the premises.

They then uncovered a collection of passports from various nationalities, including several from the US. They also found materials for and evidence of fraudulent passport manufacturing production. In all, the police detained five individuals in the house.

The scene also yielded firearms and ammunition.

The evidence later showed that three of the detainees were engineers who were trying to work on a mobile phone battery that could last many days as another way to make money.

As none of us have one of those yet, they obviously did not succeed.

In a more disturbing find, the police located an industrial-size freezer, stark and out of place. When they looked inside, they discovered dismembered human remains.

Wrapped in thick black plastic

When law enforcement officers first opened the thick black plastic bags stored in the freezer, they initially couldn't identify their contents.

Then they found a hand. And a torso. And feet with shoes still on, which strikingly underscored the human aspect of the remains.

The RTP's first task was to catalog the freezer's contents. Each body part had been wrapped with a care that was unsettling in its precision.

The body parts were sent to forensic pathologists and handled to maintain the integrity of the evidence *and* with a reverence appropriate to the sanctity of human remains.

As each body part thawed, forensic investigators documented every detail: the precise nature of the cut marks on the bones, which hinted at the tools used; the state of preservation; and any other minutiae that might silently recount the final moments of the victim's life.

There wasn't a wallet to help identify the body. The passports we found were our only clues to anyone's identity.

When the RTP called me in, my role wasn't to examine the clothes or other evidence; it was to help identify the suspect using the passports and the body. I sent a fingerprint card to the FBI lab, but given the condition of the body, I wasn't confident we would find a match.

We received the results within hours, which significantly bolstered our reputation with the RTP as the go-to agency for rapid forensic analysis.

When I reached out to the FBI lab, they confirmed what I had suspected: the advanced decomposition of the body made the prints too degraded to be of use.

As the team worked to assemble the body, they noticed the presence of blond hair, suggesting the victim was likely Western, not Thai.

If we'd had no luck in the first few days of the identification process, as a backup, we considered conducting a dental exam to investigate the victim's extensive dental work, theorizing it might help identify him due to the significant procedures he had undergone. Fortunately we identified him quickly, and we avoided the cumbersome task of reviewing dental records for Western men from the years preceding the man's disappearance.

By the end of the day, the gravity of the discovery had made headlines, with the *Bangkok Post* reporting on the frozen body found during the fake passport bust.

The FBI's advanced forensic techniques and resources

To be clear, I was never at the crime scene. Aod wasn't either. He served as the liaison officer between the scene officers and me on the first day. After that, I started working directly with the case officers who were more deeply involved in the investigation than Aod, including a future Chief of Police. Unsurprisingly, this officer had attended the FBI National Academy, which is known for building strong ties with international law enforcement leaders.

I was initially called because US passports had been found on the scene. Discovering human remains after the fact only highlighted the need to determine their legitimacy urgently. The severed limbs and preserved fragments demanded the most sophisticated scientific tools. Processing them and the passports required the advanced forensic techniques and resources housed within the FBI. Aod and the RTP needed the help of the FBI now more than ever.

When I was first called in to help, my objectives were threefold: to help identify the men arrested at the scene, to uncover the identity of the dismembered victim, and to help unravel the sequence of events that led to such a brutal and calculated act.

The passports discovered at the scene became invaluable. They were the only items with clear identifying information and photos of the suspects, which gave us a solid starting point. Even if we didn't have anything else, those passports confirmed we had grounds for passport fraud violations, so we knew we weren't wasting our time with these suspects.

And the fact that the main suspect felt compelled to shoot at the police, a highly unusual event in Thailand when it involves a foreigner shooting at Thai officers, further solidified that he was worth pursuing. While firearm violence is unfortunately common in Thailand, a foreigner resorting to such action against law enforcement is particularly rare, making him a priority in our investigation.

The suspects: two Americans and a Brit?

I delved into the complex investigation, beginning with the passports. The information on two of the US passports was legit: they belonged to two of the suspects and confirmed they were American citizens. They were identified as Aaron Thomas Gabel and James Douglas Eger.

That was the most straightforward part of the investigation. Determining the true identity of the main suspect proved far more complicated due to the large number of passports from various jurisdictions. The multitude of documents made it challenging to pinpoint which identity, if any, was legitimate.

Working closely with Tom VanDenBrink, the Regional Security Officer at the US Embassy, we dissected the layers of this complex case. VanDenBrink's expertise was crucial, especially when dealing with the intricacies of passport verification and international security protocols.

(Since then, we have presented this case at conferences, highlighting the seamless integration of field operations, back-office analysis, and the amazing partnership I shared with Tom and other members of the US law enforcement community at the Embassy.)

With VanDenBrink's help, we determined one of the passports had a legitimate British passport number and belonged to the alleged shooter. Upon further investigation, we quickly discovered that the shooter had several known aliases from many different countries. His passport was issued under the name Peter Andrew Colter, but it was likely a forgery, as the identification number was also associated with the name William Peter Johnson. His reluctance to speak only compounded the mystery.

Our breakthrough came when a fingerprint taken directly from the shooter was linked to an application for a sensitive position at a US Department of Energy national laboratory. It revealed the name Herbert Craig La Fon, an American expatriate (not British, like his passport indicated) who had been previously arrested for credit card fraud in Maryland and then blended seamlessly into the shadows of Bangkok's bustling expatriate community. His ability to evade detection was remarkable. He had lived almost invisibly at the fringes of Thai society for years.

It wasn't the first time we had seen that name; La Fon was one of the names on the passports collected at the scene. Through further investigation, we discovered Herbert Craig La Fon was the same person as Peter Andrew Colter and William Peter Johnson.

When I told Tom about the discovery, he googled Herbert Craig La Fon and found an FBI Most Wanted poster. This indicated a significant oversight in my initial checks: he was flagged by the FBI, and I had missed it.

Embarrassed by this discovery, I immediately investigated further. The only reference to the wanted poster Tom forwarded was on a niche site selling memorabilia. It was not an official FBI resource. I was confused, so I reached out to the Baltimore FBI office, the office referenced on the FBI Most Wanted poster, despite it being the middle of the night there, knowing that the Bureau's operations run around the clock. The agent I contacted helped clarify the situation: the charges against Craig had been dropped after the death of a key witness, which explained the absence of current warrants under his name and why the poster was not in official circulation.

Identifying Herbert Craig La Fon marked a significant turning point; it flung open new investigative pathways, prompting deeper inquiries and extensive searches. Knowing the identity of the shooter provided a tangible link to the murder and dismemberment of the unknown victim because it helped piece together his last days.

The victim

With the help of the FBI, the RTP had the identity of the shooter.

But we still needed to identify the victim, so Tom and I returned to the evidence collected at the scene, including an array of stolen or fake passports.

We had confirmed the identities on three of the passports, Aaron Thomas Gabel, James Douglas Eger, and Herbert Craig La Fon, but what about all the rest? Maybe one of them had a clue.

So Tom and I huddled around his computer digging through the tangled web of identities tied to the case. Tom proposed we focus on the foreign passports first, hypothesizing they might belong to *real* individuals whose identities had been stolen or misused. This approach led us to realize early on that the name Peter Andrew Colter, allegedly used by the shooter, belonged to an actual British citizen, according to our British counterparts who confirmed the passport was stolen.

As we sifted through the names on the various passports, one in particular caught our attention: Charles Edward

Ditlefsen. Tom managed to pull up Ditlefsen's passport on the State Department database, and comparing the passport photo with the haunting image of the frozen body's head of blond hair, we couldn't help but notice striking similarities in facial features...even the teeth.

But it wasn't enough to go on, and it felt like the case might have stalled.

Then, the case caught a lucky break.

I was at my desk when a close contact from the Royal Thai Police called about the case we were working on. He wanted to know if the FBI lab could analyze clothing from the crime scene to trace where it was purchased based on a brand name. It could potentially lead them to the buyer, as it had with other materials in past cases.

I immediately called Ernie Weyand, who had extensive experience with our lab, to see if it was possible. But before he could respond, I received and reviewed the photos of the clothing and noticed the name DITLE was written on the tags, similar to how names are marked on kids' clothing for camp.

When we looked at the shirt in greater detail, we found a logo: CEDCO, which we later discovered stood for the Charles Edward Ditlefsen Company.

This clue was pivotal. It led us to further dig into Ditlefsen's background, uncovering his involvement in a lawsuit in California, with the very company listed on the T-shirt.

It turned out we didn't need any further lab analysis; the victim's name was literally on the clothing, making it a straightforward clue that had initially been overlooked.

To cement our findings, we contacted Ditlefsen's sister in Los Angeles for a DNA comparison. The results were conclusive and confirmed our suspicions beyond doubt. We had found our victim.

The motive

This breakthrough, however, was just the beginning. The question of why Ditlefsen was killed was still unanswered.

So we dug deeper, and our investigation revealed that La Fon was believed to have significant financial troubles. Further, we learned of La Fon's deep personal connections in the expatriate community in Thailand. Known figures from this community, including Vietnam War-era veterans, often frequented the same bars and social circles as our suspect.

There's not much we can definitively say about the motive, as La Fon didn't reveal much during the investigation. While we couldn't confirm that La Fon was in debt, we strongly suspected that money was a driving factor. A basic look into Ditlefsen's life could easily give the impression that he was wealthy, which was not the reality. This illusion of affluence might have been enough to tempt La Fon, leading him to believe there was more to gain than there actually was.

The exact cause of Ditlefsen's death was hard to determine due to the advanced decomposition of the body, believed to have been dead for about eight years at the time of discovery. While La Fon was sentenced to close to 44 years for related crimes, the murder itself remained a mystery. He only admitted to placing the body in the freezer.

A high-level of diplomatic synergy

Once the suspect was securely in custody, the Thai judicial system sprang into action. He was tried under Thai law. The trial, held in a Thai court, became a focal point of cultural and procedural learning.

The impact of the evidence was profound, ultimately

guiding the proceedings to a decisive conclusion: the conviction of the suspect, Herbert Craig La Fon, who was sentenced to almost 44 years in prison.

While much of my time in Thailand involved navigating the differences between our two countries, things like evidence collection, the absence of jury trials, and the complexities of dual criminality, this case stood out as one of the most seamless investigations I was part of. The way the Royal Thai Police conducted themselves, the swift justice delivered, and the level of coordination we achieved made this case especially memorable during my time overseas.

For eight years, nobody was looking for Ditlefsen, not even his sister. It just goes to show, even if you're not some high-profile target, and even if nobody's actively searching, the FBI and our global partners are always ready to step in when needed. We're always out there, keeping an eye on things. This case proved that no matter how much time has passed or how rough the situation gets, we're still in the fight. It's about showing up, tracking down the truth, and standing up for justice, making sure that even when all seems lost, law enforcement is still on call.

Epilogue: Beyond the FBI

Another part of legat life I absolutely loved was the interaction I had with law enforcement officers from all over the world. Just like the US has what we call the Alphabet Police—CIA, FBI, HSI, USSS, DEA, and others—stationed at embassies around the globe, many other countries maintain a similar international law enforcement footprint.

In Bangkok, we had representatives from the Australian Federal Police, the Royal Canadian Mounted Police, the UK's

Serious Organized Crime Agency (which later became the National Crime Agency), and police services from Japan, Korea, New Zealand, Germany, France, and at least 20 other nations. It was a pretty incredible group.

For the most part, our missions were similar: to work cases that had ties back to our home countries or involved our citizens living in or visiting Thailand. That meant our cases often overlapped, whether we were investigating child exploitation, terrorism threats, fugitive apprehension, or any number of other cross-border crimes.

Some law enforcement officers had zero interest in working with the broader international law enforcement community in Thailand. That wasn't me. My experience was much richer because I leaned into those relationships. And that's largely thanks to FANC.

FANC stands for the Foreign Anti-Narcotic and Crime Community of Thailand. It's an organization made up of non-Thai law enforcement officers stationed in Bangkok. Some members were based solely in Thailand, while others covered multiple countries in the region. When I was involved, FANC served two main purposes.

First, we met regularly to discuss cases of mutual interest, share intel on crime trends across Southeast Asia, and troubleshoot challenges we might be having with local partnerships or case coordination.

Second...well, the social side of things. Let's not pretend cops don't enjoy a beer after work. FANC meetings typically ended with a few rounds, or sometimes more than a few. And as with my experience working with the Royal Thai Police, that informal time together built stronger relationships, deeper trust, and a greater sense of camaraderie.

Those nights out didn't just make the job more enjoyable;

they made us better partners. Some of my closest friends today, even after retirement, are people I met through FANC.

That consultant life

After retiring from the FBI, I didn't just step away from the world of law enforcement and security. Instead, I found a new way to use my experience, diving into the life of a consultant. I was eager to explore different opportunities, though I wasn't sure which path I wanted to commit to just yet. Then COVID-19 hit, bringing everything to a halt. The pandemic forced me to slow down (those who know me well know I can never really slow down), but it also gave me some time to think carefully about my next moves.

Even with the world slowing down, my background in navigating the Thai legal system and tracking fugitives became something that legal firms really valued. They started seeking me out for cases where a deep understanding of law enforcement techniques was crucial. My work wasn't just about finding people; it was about making sure justice could happen, even across international borders.

Around the same time, I got involved with a company focused on promoting forensic DNA technology around the world. What started as a part-time gig quickly turned into something bigger. I worked with Thai police and international agencies, helping them adopt DNA technology to solve crimes more effectively and with greater scientific accuracy. It was about taking cutting-edge science and making it practical for law enforcement.

One of the most rewarding parts of my post-FBI career has been my work in educational outreach. I started giving talks at local international schools, talking to students about the real-world consequences of risky behaviors like underage drinking and drug use. I didn't lecture them about what they should or shouldn't do. Instead, I explained the potential legal and personal consequences of their choices. This approach really resonated with both the students and the educators, and it led to more opportunities, including speaking to parents about the challenges their kids are facing today.

To stay connected with the security profession, I joined ASIS International, the world's largest organization of security professionals. As a member, and also when I was honored to be selected and serve as Chair, I've had the chance to influence global security practices, sharing insights that blend traditional law enforcement methods with modern security challenges.

My work with ASIS led me to even more rewarding opportunities in the world of security. In 2025, I became an investor and board member at Lares Risk Management, a boutique risk management and security consulting firm with a global footprint. At Lares, my skills and background fit perfectly; it will be a good retirement fit for years to come.

These various roles have kept me deeply involved in the law enforcement and security community. They've allowed me to build a bridge between my past as an FBI agent and my current work, focused on enhancing safety and security on a global scale, and given me the chance to mentor younger professionals in the field.

My life after the FBI is proof that you can continue to make a difference long after you've retired the badge.

Retirement in Thailand

It's a common belief in many jobs across America that once someone retires, the organization will crumble without them. This is especially true in the FBI, where many agents feel that they are irreplaceable, convinced that the agency can't function in their absence. FBI agents are a dedicated and intelligent group; they could have pursued careers in medicine, law, engineering, or business, but they chose the FBI.

Now, some might say this belief comes from a bit of narcissism or an inflated sense of self-importance. But the reality is the FBI has been around for over a century and keeps on running smoothly even after people retire. Cases get reassigned, and the agency continues. This is something you see across various sectors, not just in law enforcement.

The day you retire, it's almost like you were never there. Life at the FBI goes on.

In contrast, in Thailand, police titles stick with you even after retirement. For example, retired police officers are still called Police General. This respect for former titles extends to former Prime Ministers as well. They're still recognized by their previous titles, even if they served in other roles, like in the police force earlier in their careers.

Similarly, just as former US Presidents are still called President after they leave office, in Thailand, I'm still treated as an FBI agent, even though I'm retired. When I'm with my friends from the police force and introduced as John from the FBI, they always acknowledge my past role, which adds to the respect and recognition I experience in this community.

This ongoing recognition is just one of the unique aspects of living in Thailand that makes it so rewarding. Since retiring in 2019, I'm still considered the go-to expert in Thailand by my FBI colleagues and others who need security advice. That's why I am continuously called in to help, even though I retired on November 27, 2019.

Whether it's for professional consulting or just as a favor, staying this connected keeps my retirement active and fulfilling.

A strong support system

You might not realize it, but being an FBI agent often means being on call 24/7, and it was always hard to just switch off when I got home. Having a strong support system was absolutely essential.

Unlike in the US, where you might clock out at 5:00 or 6:00 p.m., unless there's an emergency, the time difference in Thailand meant my day stretched far into the night when I was Legat Bangkok. When I was getting ready for bed, the FBI in America was just starting their day. It wasn't unusual for my workday to run from the time I woke up at 6:00 or 7:00 a.m. until I went to sleep. I constantly received emails, some urgent, giving me a heads-up about what was coming next. This meant I often started my day already knee-deep in work, whether I was in transit or sitting down for breakfast. My phone was constantly buzzing with communications.

When I met my wife during training for my job with the Commerce Department, she already knew what life in federal service was like. She started her career with the DEA as an analyst, spending her days alongside DEA agents, and she got a firsthand look at the exhausting schedules they kept, especially during surveillance operations. With her background in forensic science, she understood and appreciated the demands of law enforcement work from the beginning. From the start of our now over 25 years of marriage, she's never questioned my schedule or commitments. She just gets it.

Our son, though, saw things a bit differently. We moved to Thailand when he was young, and he didn't see the action-packed side of my job. To him, I was just a dad behind a desk, which didn't seem all that impressive, even though others might have found it intriguing. I always wanted to impress him with the cool aspects of being an FBI agent, something I thought was like being a movie hero. It wasn't until he hit his teenage years that he began to understand what I do, especially as he started to grasp the significance of the stories I shared that often seemed straight out of the FBI movies he loved.

Having a family that understands the peculiarities of this job has been my backbone, making sure I can do my work effectively without any hesitation. It's a support system that not everyone in law enforcement is lucky enough to have, and it's made all the difference in helping me manage the relentless demands of my career.

Why Thailand is home

Today, I find myself reflecting on why I've made Thailand my home. This question emerges naturally for those who've journeyed through this book, witnessing my experiences. After a 10-year career with the FBI in Thailand and over 15 years in the country, some might wonder if I miss the United States. It's common for FBI agents to serve overseas and return with fond memories, eagerly resuming life in the United States. However, I belong to the smaller group who fall in love with living abroad and choose to stay.

For me, the reasons are twofold: work and family. My son attended an international school here that we absolutely loved. The quality of education he received was exceptional, and at the time of this writing, he's currently in college in the US.

When he was 17, questions arose about whether I'd return to the US after he graduated high school. But the lifestyle we've established here, including the cost of living and the community we've become part of, anchors us.

Many of my friends can't imagine leaving their hometowns, where most Americans spend their entire lives. Unlike them, my concept of home has been fluid. Growing up outside of Columbia, Maryland, halfway between Washington and Baltimore, and from my early days in the Border Patrol in Sierra Vista, Arizona, through my time in Chicago with the Commerce Department, home was always where I was *at the moment*.

But from the first time I landed at Suvarnabhumi Airport in Bangkok, something clicked. That first trip to Thailand was all I needed.

Here, helping solve crime, among lifelong friends and the vibrant city life, I truly feel at home.

BUCKSHOT

(BONUS CHAPTER)

WANT A LITTLE MORE?

This bonus chapter is for all the true crime junkies who can't get enough: a mix of short cases I've picked out that show a little extra Thai grit and grime.

The cases you'll find in this chapter aren't headline-makers or high-stakes manhunts. They're the gritty, twisty, and often surprising cases that show the hidden, day-to-day work of law enforcement. It's true crime without the glamor.

From fraudulent passports to anonymous death threats, these short stories reveal the creativity, patience, and occasional dark humor that come with the badge.

A fake Syrian passport

Our Brazilian office got a tip. FBI authorities were working in coordination with Brazilian officials to investigate a criminal organization that was involved in manufacturing fraudulent passports. This group was linked to the creation of false documents that were used by known terrorists. The operation aimed to disrupt the group's activities by targeting the source of the counterfeit passports, which posed a significant security threat due to their potential use in facilitating terrorist movements across borders.

The Brazilian FBI office raided a house and seized several computers. In collaboration with Brazilian authorities, they analyzed the passports they found on the seized computers. Among the documents, they found a Syrian passport. After further investigation, they discovered that the individual with this passport was listed on the roster of a Thai professional soccer team.

Naturally, they wondered, *Who is this guy, and why is*

his passport connected to a group making fake passports for terrorists?

The player was Venezuelan, but the passport he had was Syrian, which immediately raised another red flag:

Why would a Venezuelan soccer player need a Syrian passport?

So they sent his information to me, instructing me to find the player and figure out why his passport was linked to these computers.

Those are the only details I know about the raid, as I wasn't directly involved. My role was limited to figuring out why this particular passport ended up on the computer of a known terrorist facilitation group. This new information made the authorities keen to explore any potential Thai connection.

I got the sense that they were even considering the possibility that the soccer player might have ties to terrorism.

First, I did a little research and discovered that previously, the team had publicly announced that the player had acquired a Syrian passport because of the time his father spent in Syria.

The article I read only added to my confusion because I knew that wasn't how passports worked.

So I tracked him down.

I coordinated with the Thai police to get in touch with the management of the soccer team (or football team, as it's known in Thailand) to obtain the player's contact information. I reached out to him directly, but as you'd expect, he was pretty shocked to hear from the FBI. Over the phone, I made sure to reassure him that he wasn't in any trouble, though, in the back of my mind, I knew there was a very slim chance that he could have been involved in something suspicious. But I was 99.9999% sure he wasn't.

We arranged to meet at a hotel.

When we met, it was in the lobby of a five-star hotel. He had brought his wife and child. I sat down with him and a Thai police officer and told him he wasn't in trouble but that I needed to understand why he had a Syrian passport.

"When I first arrived in Thailand to train, the team manager handed me the Syrian passport and said, 'From now on, use this.'"

I wasn't stunned to learn that he had no connection to Syria whatsoever. I did my homework before contacting the player and went into our meeting thinking soccer might be the reason behind the passport issue, but I wasn't sure how it all fit together.

It turned out that Thai soccer teams in the top Thai professional division are allowed a quota of four foreign players. The best and most talented players in Thailand play in that league. They make the most money and have the most lucrative TV deals.

However, at the time of the incident, the rules stated these teams were allowed four foreign players in total: three foreign players from any country plus the other allocation for a player from Asia.

His Thai Premier League (T1) team already had three foreign players and couldn't recruit him as a Venezuelan, so they handed him a fraudulent *Syrian* passport and told him to say he was from Syria while in Thailand.

He claimed every team does this. They give players, often darker-skinned ones like him, fake passports and insist they pass as being from Asia.

That admission caught me off guard. I hadn't expected

the violation to be so blatant. My Thai police colleague was equally surprised at how openly the corruption was handled, without even trying to make it look legitimate.

I asked again for clarity, "So you have no ties to Syria at all?"

"None," he replied. "I've never even been to Syria."

"The team claims your father spent time in Syria."

"It's a lie."

After gathering all the information, I gave it to the Thai police and suggested they share it with the Thai Football Association (Thai FA).

And I washed my hands of it.

A pretty light day at the office.

Death threat

We received a letter one day in our Bangkok office. It was addressed to the Legat Bangkok, meaning me.

When I opened it, it was what you'd imagine a classic hostage letter would look like. It was almost like one of those movie-style ransom notes, though not quite as dramatic as one with letters cut out of magazines. It was handwritten in broken English, and the message was bizarre: the writer threatened to kill a famous Chinese actress unless the FBI fixed all the world's problems.

Not a specific problem. *All* of them.

Included with the letter was a hand-drawn map of the author of the letter's location. He claimed to live above his mother's laundromat, located in Bangkok's Chinatown, down a narrow side soi (street) where most local businesses catered to the neighborhood residents. The area was densely packed, with many families living in a small, tight-knit community.

He invited the FBI to visit once the world's problems were fixed.

This was an unusual and complex threat that we could not act on directly because we had no access to China or the actress involved.

At the time, the FBI had no working relationship with Chinese law enforcement in Thailand. It still doesn't. While we maintained strong connections with several other countries, such as Australia, New Zealand, and Germany, with whom we regularly exchanged intelligence, the Chinese authorities were not part of that network.

My immediate concern was determining the appropriate course of action. The individual making the threats was unstable, which made his behavior unpredictable. Although it was unlikely that he would act on his threats, there remained a possibility that he might.

I researched the actress, and as expected, she was a prominent figure in Chinese entertainment. But ultimately, this wasn't a case for me or the FBI to investigate directly. My research was limited to gathering initial information to determine the severity of the threat. I confirmed that the actress hadn't traveled to Thailand recently and was not currently in the country. With no immediate danger in Thailand, my role was to ensure that the information reached the right authorities.

I did not conduct in-depth research to verify the letter writer's personal details, as my primary objective was to hand off the information to the appropriate authorities. It was up to the Chinese or Thai police to investigate further based on the information I shared.

Like I already mentioned, connecting with the Chinese

government in an effort to warn the Chinese actress about the threat was a bit trickier.

During my time in Thailand, being good at my job was crucial, but sometimes, I also needed a bit of luck. And more often than not, that luck came through when I needed it most. This was definitely one of those times.

A few weeks later, I was invited to a Thai police ceremony where findings from a study on child sex trafficking were being presented. While the event was unrelated to the case at hand, it was attended by numerous officials and diplomats. I asked Aod whether any Chinese officers would be present. He confirmed that one had been invited.

Recognizing this as a potential opportunity, I first contacted the appropriate officials to brief them on my plan. I emphasized that this was not a matter of espionage or counterintelligence but a direct threat against a celebrity's life. I had already notified the Thai police, but like us, their capacity to act was limited, as the actress remained in China.

My next step was obtaining the officer's business card, as we had no prior information on him.

The ceremony took place two to three weeks after I received the letter. It was held at the Royal Thai Police Headquarters in one of the large meeting rooms. In total, there were about 100 people in attendance, both Thais and foreigners. These types of ceremonies are held a few times a year, often depending on global developments. For instance, if the Trafficking in Persons (TIP) Report rated Thailand in a way they felt didn't reflect their efforts in combating trafficking that year, they might organize more events to highlight their work. The same goes for areas like environmental crimes, transnational organized crime, and cybercrime.

At the ceremony, I identified the Chinese officer from across the room; a Thai police officer I knew pointed him out to me. As the event proceeded as expected, my attention was focused on how best to approach him.

After the ceremony ended, I introduced myself to the officer and presented him with a letter outlining the situation. I explained the nature of the threat, the relevance of the map, the actress's public stature, and the fact that the Thai individual's address had been confirmed as legitimate, as I had personally visited the location to verify its existence.

The officer remained impassive, which was not unexpected.

I further attempted to establish rapport by suggesting the possibility of future cooperation on matters such as child exploitation, an issue of concern for all nations.

His response was noncommittal, perhaps giving a vague "Maybe." He did hand me his business card, albeit with some hesitation.

It became clear that he was likely an intelligence officer rather than a standard law enforcement representative.

I gave the business card to some embassy colleagues who work China matters, and that concluded my involvement. As far as I am aware, no action was ever taken on the threat, and the actress remains unharmed.

Malaysia Airlines Flight MH370

One of the more high-profile cases I worked on involved the disappearance of Malaysia Airlines Flight MH370, a case that's been in the news for years.

The flight went missing on March 8, 2014. It was en route from Kuala Lumpur, Malaysia, to Beijing, China, when it lost contact with air traffic control less than an hour after takeoff and disappeared from radar.

Despite extensive efforts, the main wreckage has never been recovered. But small pieces of debris were found on beaches on Indian Ocean islands and in eastern Africa. It's believed that the plane went down in one of the deepest parts of the Indian Ocean, where the underwater terrain is rugged, with massive underwater mountain ranges. Locating anything down there would be extremely difficult, if not impossible.

In the initial 24 hours following the plane's disappearance, authorities strongly suspected terrorism. Several stolen passports appeared on the passenger manifest, which led to the assumption that they were tied to potential terrorist activity, as stolen passports are often used in such cases.

But within 48 hours, both intelligence and law enforcement agencies began reassessing the situation. While terrorism was not entirely ruled out, investigators realized that the route from Malaysia to Beijing, and then from Beijing to Europe, was frequently used by migrants traveling to Europe for work.

Further investigation revealed that the use of fake passports along this route wasn't uncommon. Migrants often come through Southeast Asia, where it's relatively easy to obtain counterfeit documents, before continuing to Europe. So while the presence of stolen passports initially pointed to terrorism, it became more likely that the individuals using these documents were simply migrants trying to get to Europe for work.

Two of the stolen passports were reported as lost in Thailand, which brought me into the case. One was an Austrian passport and the other Italian, and both had been reported stolen in Phuket. I immediately flew down from Bangkok to investigate further.

The Austrian passport belonged to a tourist who had already left the country by the time I arrived. I reviewed the police report filed at the time of the theft, and the Austrian Embassy confirmed that the passport had been reported lost. The tourist claimed he had either been pickpocketed during his ride from the airport to his hotel or it fell out of his backpack.

Some people have asked me whether I believed him. It didn't really matter to me whether he was lying. Investigating a missing, stolen, or illegally sold Austrian passport fell under the jurisdiction of the Thai or Austrian authorities. My focus was on the missing plane. What I needed to verify was whether the passport had actually been lost or stolen in Thailand to confirm the origin of the passenger. Once I verified that the Austrian Embassy had received the report and spoken with the original passport owner, I was confident in updating those working on the MH370 case that we had traced the origin of one of the stolen passports on the flight.

The case involving the Italian passport raised more red flags. The passport belonged to a young Italian man in his twenties, still residing in Phuket at the time. Aod, an Australian Federal Police (AFP) colleague who was also assigned to look into the missing passports from the Australian government, and I arranged to meet with him, along with his lawyer, at the Italian consulate. He claimed that he had left his passport at a scooter rental shop and, upon returning to retrieve it, was told it had been lost.

But when we questioned the scooter shop, they denied any knowledge of the missing passport. They had no records indicating that it had ever been lost.

Based on this and other evidence, we began to suspect that the Italian man had sold his passport for money, a common scheme. In these cases, an individual sells their passport, reports it as stolen to their embassy, and gets a replacement. While this might go unnoticed if done once, it becomes an issue if repeated. We believe this is what happened in this case, and his passport was ultimately used by one of the passengers on MH370.

My work was done, but the FBI's was not.

Through its investigation, it uncovered the pilot was a Malaysian citizen living in Malaysia, and as a veteran pilot for Malaysian Airlines, he had extensive experience.

While much of the information that has emerged since MH370 went missing remains speculative or unconfirmed, some details have been reported through credible sources, including the FBI. According to open-source reports, the pilot had a flight simulator in his basement, which was analyzed by the FBI. The analysis revealed recent simulated flights, including one that closely mirrored the suspected flight path taken by MH370.

I'm not sure if having a flight simulator at home is standard practice for pilots, but simulators are a regular part of pilot training and job requirements.

Unconfirmed reports and interviews with anonymous colleagues of the pilot suggested that he had made inappropriate posts of a sexual and political nature on social media.

However, it's crucial to emphasize that until the plane is found, all such information remains speculative.

Poisoned

I'm retired now, yet I still remain connected to some of the law enforcement activities in Thailand. In particular, I was called in to help with a poisoning incident that occurred on July 16, 2024, at the Grand Hyatt Erawan Hotel in Bangkok.

It wasn't the Thai police who reached out to me in this instance. I became involved because of my role as Chair of the Thailand chapter of ASIS International, one of the world's largest private security organizations. (It used to be known as the American Society of Industrial Security, but with its growing international presence, it's now called ASIS International.) The organization's members range from hotel security managers to heads of corporate security for companies like Disney. When I retired, I was asked to serve as the Chair for Thailand, and I accepted.

One day, while I was at home, I received a message in the ASIS Telegram group (Telegram is a secure messaging app, much like WhatsApp or Line). A woman, the head of security for Agoda, a major travel company in Asia, had posted, asking if anyone had heard about reports of an active shooter near CentralWorld, a major shopping mall in Bangkok. Agoda's headquarters are in close proximity to that area, and she was concerned about the safety of both their employees and customers staying at nearby hotels, such as the Hyatt Erawan.

No one in the group had any information at the time, so I immediately reached out to Aod. He responded quickly, clarifying that it wasn't a shooting but a possible poisoning and that he would keep me updated.

During major events, when reports come in quickly, I need to relay what I know while new information continues to emerge. At that point, what I knew for sure was the most critical piece: this was not an active shooter situation, and the threat was almost certainly no longer present.

This distinction was critical for Agoda. If there had been an active shooter, they may have needed to issue warnings to their customers and staff to avoid the area. Knowing it was likely a poisoning, I could reassure them that it wasn't as dangerous as an active shooter situation. Nothing was 100% certain, but the available information strongly suggested that the immediate threat had passed. While the details weren't yet specific and we didn't have a full understanding of the situation, I could reasonably assume that it wasn't a "live" or active danger.

Within an hour, my contact confirmed that it was indeed a localized poisoning. The incident occurred in a guest room, with all involved either deceased in the room or nearby, and while police had not yet released specific details, they had confirmed that there was no ongoing threat to anyone outside of those already deceased. I relayed this information back to the ASIS group, and all our members were able to notify appropriate personnel.

I wanted to dig a little deeper into the situation, so I contacted a close friend of mine who still works for the FBI. She's stationed in Washington, DC, but has oversight on cases involving Thailand. I wanted to make sure the FBI was aware of what was happening.

The situation escalated when I learned that two of the victims were US citizens. Within two hours, I received the immigration records for all the victims, confirming the presence of two Americans among them.

While the poisoning itself wasn't a major FBI case and was more a matter of news, any incident involving US citizens adds a layer of importance. This shift meant it was something I needed to inform my FBI colleagues about, even though the FBI might not necessarily take the lead or be fully involved in the investigation. And as I had come across this new information very quickly after the incident, I felt a responsibility to share it with my former colleagues.

My FBI contact in Washington advised me she hadn't received any information yet, but I assumed the office would be briefed soon enough.

Eventually, I knew my need for updates would diminish as the situation developed. Now, in retirement, I remain available to support my private-sector contacts, my colleagues in the Thai police, and the FBI whenever needed.

Within a few hours it became clear that this wasn't just a simple poisoning; it was a murder-suicide. One of the Vietnamese Americans had been involved in a financial dispute. Apparently she had either lost or stolen money intended for an investment in a hospital project in Japan.

The group had gathered in Bangkok to settle the issue, but negotiations hadn't gone as planned. (They had met over the course of a few days and hadn't been able to come to a resolution.) The woman invited everyone to her hotel room for one final meeting. She ordered tea and food and insisted on preparing the tea herself. That was a notable detail since at a high-end hotel like the Hyatt Erawan, the staff would normally handle such tasks. She poisoned the tea with cyanide, killing everyone in the room, including herself.

I didn't see pictures of the victims after they died, but I did get a look at the scene. The suite at the Hyatt Erawan was still in disarray. The room was spacious, and there was a tray of food with tea and coffee cups, still untouched. Full plates of food, typical of a Thai-style shared meal with large portions, remained on the table. According to the police reports, four of the six victims were found in one room, while the other two were in another room of the suite.

Although I wasn't directly involved in the investigation, I continued passing along the information I received.

The situation wrapped up by the second day. I received updates from my RTP contacts and promptly shared the information with members of the ASIS International Thailand Chapter and my colleague at FBI HQ.

Even in retirement, I remain closely tied to ongoing situations in the region.

Each case in this chapter is a reminder of why I chose this line of work and why I'm still deeply involved in Thailand's security scene, even in retirement. Whether it's lending a hand to private-sector colleagues or keeping an eye on developments with local police, there's always work to be done.

# ACKNOWLEDGMENTS

TO MY WIFE, CARMEN. YOU ARE EVERYTHING TO ME. This journey, both in the FBI and in writing this book, would not have been the same without your love and support.

Cole, my son, may you find your passion as I did with the FBI. You may not realize it, but your support has always motivated me.

Thank you, Mom, for always being my sounding board, complaint department, and cheerleader.

To my sister, Amy. Having you by my side in Asia all these years has been (and continues to be) an incredible source of support.

And to Aod, my Thai brother. Thanks for everything. I know there are more adventures ahead.

To all the victims and their families who have lived through these stories. Your strength and dedication to justice has been incredible and has truly shaped this book. You're the heart of this story, and this book is a tribute to your resilience.

Thanks to my editor, Lisa; my book manager, Emmy; and my publisher, Scribe, for supporting me and helping bring my dream of writing this book to life.

Finally, to my father. While I've dedicated this book to your memory, I want to thank you once more for being my lifelong inspiration.

ABOUT THE AUTHOR

JOHN SCHACHNOVSKY is a retired FBI Supervisory Special Agent and former Legal Attaché at the US Embassy in Bangkok, Thailand, where he led the FBI's operations across the Southeast Asia region. Over the course of a 25-year career in law enforcement, John developed a reputation for managing complex national security operations, coordinating international criminal investigations, and building bridges between law enforcement agencies across borders.

With deep, real-world experience in intelligence gathering, counterterrorism, cybercrime, and fugitive apprehension, John has operated at the highest levels of global law enforcement. From tracking high-value targets in Africa to navigating diplomatic challenges in Southeast Asia, he has led teams through high-stakes missions in some of the world's most challenging environments.

Since retiring from the Bureau, John has remained an influential voice in the security world. As a frequent lecturer, he speaks to students, law enforcement professionals, and business leaders throughout the APEC region on topics ranging from global security trends to practical strategies in risk management. He also serves on the Board of Directors and as a Strategic Advisor at Lares Risk Management International, offering expert guidance on corporate security, intelligence, and crisis response.

In 2023, he was named Chair of ASIS International Thailand, the regional chapter of the world's largest professional organization for security management professionals.

John lives in Bangkok, which he considers home, with his wife and son. When he's not speaking or consulting, he continues to mentor the next generation of security professionals and supports initiatives that promote integrity, transparency, and law enforcement cooperation across borders.

www.ingramcontent.com/pod-product-compliance
Lightning Source LLC
Chambersburg PA
CBHW060523080526
44586CB00012B/586